the city dog

hamlyn

the city dog

THE ESSENTIAL GUIDE FOR THE URBAN OWNER

Sarah Whitehead

An Hachette Livre UK Company
www.hachettelivre.co.uk

First published in Great Britain in 2008 by
Hamlyn, a division of Octopus Publishing Group Ltd
2–4 Heron Quays, London E14 4JP
www.octopusbooks.co.uk

ISBN: 978-0-600-61724-2

A CIP catalogue record for this book is available from the
British Library.

Printed and bound in China

10 9 8 7 6 5 4 3 2 1

contents

City life is stimulating, challenging and inspiring. City dwellers know just how diverse life can be, and appreciate both the good points and the bad. However, more and more of us are realizing that our lives can be enhanced by owning companion dogs and that, with a little time and effort, they can fit into the cityscape, by our sides.

introduction

Of course, owning a dog in the city comes with a completely different set of issues from owning one that gambols in the countryside. While it may be tempting to think of most dogs being at home in green fields and woodland, they can adapt well to life in the city and can flourish there, with a little understanding, training and care. Dogs can live perfectly happily in towns and cities – indeed, there are some advantages in terms of socialization opportunities, although you need to socialize and train them with the urban environment in mind.

Living in a town or city can be a challenge for humans, let alone dogs. The sheer proximity of other people, other dogs, close neighbours and a lack of space can increase the stress and pressure on both species, and this can lead to tensions between dog owners and non-dog owners in the same community. However, this doesn't have to be the case. Your mission is to ensure that your dog contributes to the energy and enjoyment of the city, both for you and for all those whom he or she meets.

Although it may not be all green fields and open skies, it is undeniable that the city has a life-force all of its own, and there is every reason for dogs to fit right in.

If you try to see the city from your dog's point of view, you will gain an entirely different perspective of your previously familiar surroundings.

Street baby

If you live in a town or city and have recently got a puppy, there's not a minute to waste. Walking in a concrete jungle may not be as soothing as a stroll in the country, but it is paramount that you get your puppy out and about. You need to expose your dog to every possible sight, sound, smell and touch that he or she is going to need to cope with. Just think about how the world must appear to your puppy. The streets are not paved with gold, but with litter, feet and the oncoming wheels of pushchairs. Your puppy is likely to have to deal with aspects of life that a country dog may never experience. Consider the likelihood that he or she will need to ride in a lift, travel on a bus or train, or be walked next to schools where groups of children congregate. Building work, street repairs and noisy vehicles are all on your puppy's exposure checklist – missing out on encountering these things now may lead to potential stress, anxiety and fear in your dog later on.

Socializing you and your dog

Dogs tend to suffer in cities only because their owners have not considered what they need in order to be able to express their natural behaviour. Untrained and unsocialized dogs bark, leave a mess, cause havoc in the streets and create nuisance for urban neighbours. This is not through disobedience, but because no one has taught them how to behave otherwise. Taking on a dog in the city means accepting a commitment to spending time, energy and effort in doing just that. However, this is by no means an unpleasant journey. In owning a dog you will soon discover that your own experience of the city changes, too. In sharing your life with a dog you will discover new horizons to explore, new experiences to be had and a new language to learn. Prepare yourself for taking more exercise, reducing your stress levels, meeting your neighbours, talking to people in the street and making many new friends – all this in the name of your puppy's socialization!

Dogs love to learn, and they love to socialize. If you have a passion for the city, and for dogs, this is the book for you.

8

which dog?

choosing a dog that suits you

Just like people, some dogs suit city living better than others. Whether or not a breed or individual dog will fit into the urban landscape very much depends on a combination of physical and behavioural attributes and needs. In turn, these need to fit neatly with your own environment and lifestyle – making your choice of dog supremely important.

If you are considering getting a dog to live with you in the city, there are many factors to take into account. However, if you have already committed yourself to a breed or type, thinking about his needs will enable you to maximize his quality of life.

Size matters
Quite clearly, size matters in the city. This is not to say that large dogs are out of the question, but where

space, time and exercise opportunities are limited, you need to give a great deal of consideration to the practicalities involved.

Some of the large breeds require a great deal of exercise – preferably off-lead. Dogs like Labradors, for example, really need to be able to run unhindered at least twice a day for a minimum of 40 minutes. How practical this is will depend largely on the facilities available in your city – after all, some of the biggest

Toy dogs are small in stature but are often brimming with personality, a combination that makes many of them excellent city companions.

generally require less exercise, simply because they need to cover less ground to gain the same benefit. However, very small dogs are at risk of being trodden on in the street, and although 'handbag' dogs are all the rage, it is simply not fair to restrict natural canine behaviour by carrying dogs rather than allowing them to walk whenever possible.

The eye of the beholder

Being attracted to the appearance of certain breeds and not others is highly subjective. Some people think that Pugs are the epitome of beauty, while others consider them plain ugly. The sight of an Afghan Hound with its elegant, flowing coat may set some hearts aflutter, while others just see endless grooming! Of course it is important to enjoy the appearance of your chosen breed, but this should never be a top priority. Breed-specific behaviour and hard-wired (genetically driven) characteristics are far more important, because these will affect your everyday quality of life for at least 13 years. For this reason alone, it is vital that you do your research into which breeds would suit you, which would fit with ease into city life, and even which kinds of dogs are permitted to be kept in your locality.

and best parks in the world are situated cheek-by-jowl with the urban sprawl of large cities, while other urban areas can only offer one small and overcrowded dog park.

Other large breeds (especially the giant ones) do not need huge amounts of exercise, and some of them are surprisingly adaptable to small-space living, because they like to lie around rather than race about. However, their sheer physical presence on the street can be a major issue as they vie for space with pedestrians, buggies, shop fronts and café seating. Just imagine trying to negotiate the city streets on a busy morning rush hour with a St Bernard in tow!

Small dogs clearly dominate the best choices for city breeds. They are portable, affectionate and

An adult affair

When choosing a dog, always talk to people who own adult versions of the breed in question, rather than just looking at puppies. It is all too easy to get carried away looking at little bundles of fluff, when the adult reality is what you should really fall in love with.

urban myths and urban laws

Dogs and humans have lived side by side for centuries, but with the rise in urban living, more and more laws are being imposed on dog owners in order to keep communities safe and clean. Unfortunately this has resulted in a number of cities – and even whole countries – implementing restrictions on owning certain types of dog and limiting where dogs may be exercised or kept.

Breed restrictions

Although most animal-behaviour specialists dispute the aggressive tendencies of specific breeds, a disproportionate number of injuries to people have resulted in some countries and cities prohibiting the ownership of dogs such as Pit Bull Terriers and Rottweilers. Even where a complete ban has been avoided, some cities require owners to buy liability insurance, keep their dogs behind 2 m (6 ft)-high fences and muzzle them whenever they are in public. Interestingly, in many countries local laws regarding dog restrictions change from place to place, so check with someone with local knowledge if you plan to travel with your dog or are considering relocating. Below are a few examples of countries with dog restrictions.

United States

Every state in the US is permitted its own legislation regarding dogs. These may include state-wide lead laws, compulsory insurance or health regulations. Some have already passed laws governing certain breeds, and many states have lead laws relating to public areas that affect all dogs, no matter what the breed. For instance, in New York all dogs must be on leads no longer than 2 m (6 ft) in length.

Great Britain

Since 1991 Britain has had a nationwide ban on the breeding or keeping of the American Pit Bull Terrier, the Japanese Tosa and a dog of any type designated as being bred for fighting. Many cities have restrictions on where dogs can be exercised and let off-lead in certain areas, and nearly all towns have strict laws regarding dog fouling and control.

Irish Republic

Eleven breeds of dog have been banned from all Dublin City Council properties, including houses, flats and estates. The council also plans to amend its local laws to include public parks in the ban. This would mean that anyone owning what they describe as a 'dangerous dog' could not walk it in a public park, even if they lived in private housing. The breeds are: English Bull Terrier, Staffordshire Bull Terrier, American Pit Bull Terrier, Rottweiler, German Shepherd (Alsatian), Dobermann, Rhodesian Ridgeback, Japanese Akita, Bull Mastiff, Japanese Tosa and Bandog. Cross-breeds of these dogs with any other breed are also banned.

France

France recently enacted a policy requiring the neutering of all 'attack' dogs, making it impossible to breed them. Italy intends to introduce breed bans soon.

Breed-specific legislation is highly controversial, but many countries are now restricting the ownership of certain breeds – or even those that resemble them.

Germany

In Germany, as in the US, every state can pass its own legislation; many German states have placed severe restrictions on the ownership of breeds such as the Pit Bull Terrier, but the greatest restrictions are in the state of Hessen, where 16 different breeds are banned.

Iceland

In 1924 dogs were banished from Reykjavik after an outbreak of dog-related diseases. The city of 88,000 people lived without dogs until 2003, when an experiment to reintroduce them was tried. Under the terms of this, Reykjavik's 850 registered dog owners paid yearly licence fees and agreed to strict limits: no dogs were allowed in the city's central district, they had to stay out of public parks between 8 a.m. and 9 p.m. and could not enter any public building. Strict laws still apply and more restrictions may be forthcoming. Reykjavik's dog owners have protested against this legislation, which still prevents them from taking their dogs to some neighbourhoods and downtown areas.

different breeds, different needs

As a species, dogs have the most variety in terms of size, colour, coat type and appearance of any animal on the planet. However, it is not just their physical appearance that distinguishes between them. Breeds have evolved over the centuries to fulfil certain functions, and these characteristics are alive and well in our pets today.

Interestingly, few people understand that breed characteristics are directly linked to breed needs, and – ultimately – canine contentment. Despite centuries of breeding, many dogs still retain working instincts that need to be fulfilled for the dog to be happy. This means that we should choose and keep dogs that can cope with living in the city and we must create appropriate outlets for their natural behaviours.

Fashion vs function

Strong breed characteristics may be obvious in context, but few people realize that these drives are hard-wired. For example, most people would expect a Border Collie to retain the desire to herd and would anticipate that it would become excited at the sight of a flock of sheep. However, given a cityscape rather than a field, this same dog still needs to express chasing and circling behaviours – which all too often are directed at children, cyclists or joggers.

Some breeds may lull prospective owners into a false sense of security, by their appearance, general demeanour or even reputation. Cocker Spaniels may look like sweet little lapdogs, but given the chance they become lively, active workaholics, addicted to retrieving! West Highland White Terriers, Jack Russells and other terriers have far more working drive than they are often given credit for – and this needs to be channelled, if they are to make good city pets.

Finding out what your dog loves to do is partly based on breed needs and partly on individual characteristics. Making assumptions about what certain breeds can or cannot do is always risky. For example, it is not unheard of for Pugs to be great at agility, or for some Golden Retrievers to hate playing fetch. Watching your dog's body language and learning about his individual 'personality' is half the fun of being a dog owner.

Do you know what makes your dog tick? Is he exhilarated by chase games or content with cuddles? Breeds, types and individuals all have different needs.

Your dog's day

Try to think about how your dog's day will work out. Imagine a clock face. Most dogs have certain needs, such as resting, eating, playing and having contact with humans. How many hours does this take up? Depending on breed or type, the rest of the day should include specific pursuits: digging, chasing, chewing, retrieving, searching or problem-solving. It is up to you to find ways to make this happen so that the long hours are used constructively.

Those who live with dogs know that animals have moods and emotional states just as humans do – and these can be influenced by the environment and context in which a dog lives. In return, these moods affect the way the dog behaves, and even how easy he is to train. For example, can you imagine trying to train a Rhodesian Ridgeback not to bark at the front door when he has not been out for exercise for several days? How about attempting to gain your Jack Russell's attention when he can hear next door's cat miaowing for attention? Clearly, the dog's emotional state will affect his ability to concentrate, learn and control his own impulses.

Filling your dog's day with as many outlets for his natural behaviour as you can might sound challenging in the city – but it's quite possible, and it can be fun! The first step is to acknowledge what your dog needs by understanding the purpose for which he was bred. The second is to be creative and think of ways that he can actively engage in appropriate exercise (for both body and mind) that fits his breed and his needs.

behavioural and physical characteristics

If you are choosing a pedigree puppy, it's imperative to consider whether he will be happy in an urban environment. If you already have your puppy, find out what he was originally bred to do – this will enhance your understanding of your dog's behaviour and help him to fit into city life with ease.

Gundogs/Sporting

Gundogs have always made very popular pets and, on the whole, have an extremely good reputation as family dogs. Many of the gundog breeds retain strong working drives, and while this makes them easy to motivate in training, without sufficient stimulation they can easily become self-employed. The vast majority of the retrievers and spaniels in this group love to carry objects around in their mouths and will happily chew household items if a more appropriate toy is not available. Most gundogs need lots of free-running exercise and have an affinity with mud and water!

Hounds

On the whole, hounds are strong-minded. Bred to live and hunt in packs, they usually bond to their owners, but will think nothing of deserting them in favour of a scent in the city park. Many hounds – particularly the larger breeds, such as the Hamiltonstovare and the Bloodhound – have a reputation as escape-artists and can even scale high fencing. Even the smaller hounds retain an independent will, which means that all the dogs in this group require substantial early training and socialization, particularly if you want to exercise them outside off-lead.

Working and pastoral

These groups contain the herders and heelers – dogs that have been bred to help humans keep their flocks and herds together and move them from field to field, as well as other working types, such as the St Bernard and the Siberian Husky. The pastoral group contains many well-known favourites, such as the Border Collie, Briard and Rough Collie. Most of these dogs retain a great desire to herd animals and, in the absence of a flock of sheep, this may well include your children, or joggers and cyclists in urban streets. Pastoral breeds (and many of those in the working group) need a job to do, and while their original tasks may be impractical for the city dog, they are adept at learning tricks and all types of training and often excel at dog 'sports', such as flyball and agility. As puppies, all members of this group need to learn to channel their chase instinct in an appropriate way, through play with canine toys and extensive, but enjoyable training.

Terriers

Terriers have fast responses, courage and a strong survival instinct, which can mean that they appear to be feisty, stubborn and noisy – although they perceive their behaviour as fun! Many terriers are at the smaller end of the height range, so they can be mistaken for lapdogs, although nothing could be further from the truth. They need lots of socialization when young, particularly with other dogs. Intelligent, fast and reactive, terriers are loved the world over by those who like their dogs to have real 'personality'; such people are prepared to put in the time and effort to train and socialize – and be owned by – a terrier!

Toys

The toy dogs have been selectively bred to be companion dogs, and therefore many of them are small – if not tiny. However, they are often keen to take as much exercise as you can offer them and have large personalities in a small frame. The Cavalier King Charles Spaniel is probably the most popular breed in this group, possessing an enthusiasm for life that is highly infectious and a hardy outlook in a conveniently

Toy dogs, such as the Bichon Frise make excellent family pets. Their coats can be easily maintained in a pet clip.

compact package. Many of the toy breeds are also highly trainable. The Pomeranian, Papillon and ever-popular Yorkshire Terrier are more than capable of being trained to a high level for many of the sports designed for 'minis', such as agility and obedience.

Utility/Non-sporting

This group represents a rather ill-defined selection of breeds. On the whole, most 'utility' dogs have found themselves out of work, because the job they were originally bred to do is no longer in existence. The Dalmatian, for instance, was bred to run behind horse-drawn carriages. Several spitz-type dogs are also in this group: the Akita, smaller Shiba Inu and the Japanese and German Spitz all show the curled tail carriage so typical of this type of dog. They retain some basic instincts, such as hunting and protective behaviour, making early training and socialization imperative.

pros and cons of different breeds

GUNDOGS/SPORTING	PROS	CONS
Labrador Retriever	Short, easy-care coat; equable family pet	Lively when young; needs lots of training and exercise
Cocker Spaniel	Good size for the city; cheerful and lively	Still needs to chase and retrieve; requires professional grooming
Italian Spinone	A large dog, but calm as an adult	The coat is tough and wiry and can be odorous; has a tendency to slobber

HOUNDS	PROS	CONS
Basset Hound	Short coat, moderate exercise required	Adults are quite large, heavy dogs; may have health problems
Petit Basset Fauve de Bretagne	Good size for the city; bright and trainable	Needs significant amounts of exercise; has the hound tendency to be distracted by scent
Miniature Dachshund	A loving, sporting pet	Can be sensitive, both physically and mentally, so caution is needed with small children; beware back problems

WORKING AND PASTORAL	PROS	CONS
Shetland Sheepdog	Affectionate and gentle	Its long coat needs considerable grooming; requires lots of early socialization to gain confidence in the city; can be sound-sensitive
Pinscher	A compact, stylish, adaptable medium-sized dog	Can be noisy; dislikes rough handling, so caution is needed with children
Corgi	Smart, alert and a good size for city living; its short coat needs limited grooming	The propensity to bark is instinctive; needs lots of motivation in training as it can be strong-willed

TERRIERS	PROS	CONS
West Highland White Terrier	Attractive, smart little dog with an outgoing temperament	Don't be fooled by this dog's diminutive size – he needs lots of training and socialization to prevent him being noisy or snappy; professional grooming required
Bedlington Terrier	Lamb-like in appearance, but with a real lust for life	The coat requires regular trimming; needs plenty of exercise and stimulation

TOYS	PROS	CONS
Pomeranian	Bright, lively, but pocket-sized; loves to be with people	Needs company and lots of grooming
Bichon Frise	Happy and cheerful, as well as glamorous	Professional grooming required
Yorkshire Terrier	A big dog in a small frame	Professional clipping/grooming required; may not be very tolerant of the attentions of small children
Chihuahua	Smooth or long-coated, so a choice of grooming needs; pocket-sized and affectionate	Not suitable with young children; some 'protection' needed in the city or it can easily be trodden on or injured

UTILITY/ NON-SPORTING	PROS	CONS
Boston Terrier	Bright and keen, this little dog has the 'bull breed' look	Quite boisterous, and needs plenty of mental and physical stimulation
French Bulldog	Huge bat ears make this dog distinctive; it is compact and short-coated, with lots of character	Can suffer from hereditary problems and breathing complaints, especially in the heat
Poodle	Bred in three sizes, Poodles are intelligent and active, with a non-shedding coat	Professional grooming required; needs lots of training and exercise (even the toy and miniature versions)
Shih Tzu	Bouncy, outgoing and cheerful; an ideal, compact size for the city	Much grooming required

'designer dogs'

Breeds have changed dramatically over the past century. Where dogs were once prized for their working abilities, most are now bred for their looks or companionship – effectively making many breeds 'unemployed' or unsuitable solely as pets, particularly in the city. First-crosses or 'designer dogs' are therefore coming into their own, enabling owners to enjoy a combination of two sets of inherited characteristics.

The new breeds about town

The first-cross is the result of a planned mating between two pedigree breeds. This can work well for city living, because an ideal-sized breed such as a Jack Russell can be bred with a dog with less working instinct, such as a Cavalier King Charles Spaniel, which – at least in theory – will result in the best of both characteristics.

However, one word of warning: there is no guarantee that the first-cross of your dreams will turn out to be a perfect balance of his parents' attributes. Despite sometimes huge price-tags, even characteristics like colour and coat length can vary enormously in puppies from the same litter, and factors such as whether or not they shed hair can never be assured in advance. This makes choosing a deliberate first-cross a bit of a lottery, although it is guaranteed that you will end up with a truly unique dog!

What's in a name?

Queen Elizabeth II of England may have been one of the first breeders to name a 'designer breed', after one of her Corgis mated with her sister's Dachshund; the resulting puppies were called 'Dorgis'. One of the most wonderful aspects of owing a 'designer dog' is that the names given to them are so apt and, frequently, amusing. The Pekepoo (a cross between a Pekingese and a Poodle), the Muggin (a combination of Miniature Pinscher and Pug) and the Snorkie (a Miniature Schnauzer/Yorkshire Terrier mix) all conjure up images every bit as intriguing as the dogs' looks.

The results of a first cross between a Pug and a Beagle. While Puggles may not be everyone's cup of tea, they are certainly distinctive!

Labradoodle

The best known of all the first-crosses, the Labradoodle is a cross between a pedigree Labrador and a Poodle. It was originally bred to work as a service dog, with the idea that it could be placed with blind people who had allergies to the usual shedding coats of such dogs. The appearance of the Labradoodle can vary greatly – from short-coated and black to curly and blond. Its behaviour is often variable, too: some seem laid-back and affable, while others are prone to excitement and barking. Not all are non-shedding.

Puggle

The Puggle is a relatively new and popular cross-breed, bringing together the Pug and the Beagle. It is no surprise that combining the characteristics and features of an energetic hound and a loving lapdog is proving very popular. Puggles are typically energetic, sweet-tempered, loving, intelligent and playful. The short, smooth coat may be fawn, tan, white and black, or a mixture. Puggles often have a short, wrinkled muzzle – taking after the Pug – although this varies, and beauty is very definitely in the eye of the beholder!

Cockapoo

This is a cross between a Cocker Spaniel and a Poodle (usually a miniature one). Cockapoos have been bred for some years, but still vary greatly in colour and coat type. Indeed, it is not uncommon to find tight-curled, wavy-haired and flat-coated puppies in the same litter. These little dogs tend to be outgoing and cheerful, and usually have their coats clipped into a 'teddy bear' style for ease of maintenance.

choosing a dog from a rescue centre

As many owners discover, getting a dog from a rescue centre or welfare organization can be the very best place to start – not a last resort. Many dogs are given up for adoption through no fault of their own: the pressure of city life can take its toll on pets as well as families, and dogs fall on hard times when their owners develop allergies, split up or have to move and cannot take them along.

Great expectations

So, just how are you going to select a dog from all those cute faces and sorrowful eyes? Choosing a dog is like choosing a partner – select on looks alone and you will quickly be disappointed – so think about what you want in a pet *before* you go to a rehoming centre.

Of course, the advantage of choosing a rescue dog is that many are often adult, or adolescent, leaving no surprises as to their eventual size and coat length. This can be of particular benefit in city living, where you don't really want to find that your neat little urban pup turns into a hairy monster that dominates your tiny apartment. However, even if the dog that attracts you is a cross-breed, consider the likelihood of breed tendencies and how its parentage may influence its behaviour. For example, hound-crosses will undoubtedly like tracking and sniffing, while Labrador-crosses will probably need a good deal of exercise and time spent training.

Spend time just watching all the dogs in the kennel before choosing. Positive signs of good temperament and sociability are easy to confuse with over-excitement and stress. Tail wagging does not always mean friendliness, and barking does not always constitute a threat.

Children and dogs can be best buddies, but ideally the dog you choose must really love being with kids.

❋ If you have children, he enjoys their company and contact. Your pet will need to love being around children, and not just tolerate them.

Bad signs

❋ The dog stands still or rigid and barks at you from a little way back in the kennel.

❋ He shows you his teeth, or stares at you with direct eye contact.

❋ He 'mouths' you (puts his mouth on you as if to bite, but without any pressure from his teeth) even if it's 'only in play'.

❋ He ignores you. Don't be fooled by the idea that the dog has been cooped up in a kennel and therefore finds everything else distracting – if he's sociable, he will be thrilled to have a human being pay him attention. If you stroke him, he should ask for more, not move away.

❋ Do *not* choose a dog just because he looks cute or reminds you of one that you have known!

When you have chosen a dog, ask if you can take him out, but don't just take him for a walk. Sit down with him so that you can observe his behaviour and see how quickly he settles and how much he enjoys just being with you – this should be the start of a beautiful relationship, so take the time to make sure it's right.

Good signs

❋ When in the kennel, the dog wants to approach you and make contact by pressing his muzzle or body against the bars. If you move your hand, does the dog follow and try to maintain contact?

❋ The dog's body looks soft and flexible.

❋ His facial expression is 'soft', while eye contact is often squinty (he narrows his eyes to look appeasing).

❋ His tail goes round and round (usually an indication of excitement) rather than in low, quick wags (which may indicate uncertainty).

❋ Once out of the kennel, the dog gives you his attention. Social dogs will want to solicit your attention and interact.

Second chance

Older dogs or even elderly ones can be hugely rewarding and can easily fit into an urban daily routine. They often have a 'second puppyhood' when given a new chance at life in a loving home, and take up less time than an unruly puppy.

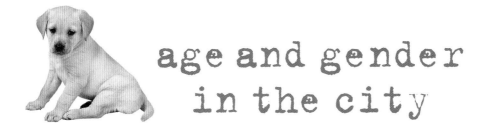

age and gender in the city

It's easy to think of city life as being for the young. A city pup – bright and bouncy, but with so much to learn – needs to be exposed to all the stimulation the urban environment has to offer; his ability to cope with your lifestyle will be established now. However, it's important to consider how fast-paced urban living can affect your dog at any age. Adolescents and seniors can fit right in, too.

Teenage rebel

We accept that our children will enter a teenage phase, where they test boundaries and experiment with their own behaviour, and the same can be true for dogs. Hormonal changes, rapid growth and a sense of their own independence will lead dogs to push you (and possibly other dogs), simply to test the water.

At this stage, male dogs may feel the need to square up to other male dogs they meet, and this can

become a learned habit if it is allowed to continue – a particularly antisocial and potentially dangerous problem in the city. Depending on the veterinary practice, neutering is generally advised at around six months to one year old.

Female dogs generally first come into season at 7–14 months. The first signs are that the bitch urinates more frequently outdoors as she leaves her scent for male dogs to follow. During their season, female dogs become highly attractive to male dogs and may be tense around other bitches – this means that taking them out can become highly problematic, especially if there are stray dogs around. Most veterinary opinion now supports neutering female dogs before their first season, or three months after it to prevent unwanted litters of puppies.

Senior years

Generally, small dogs tend to live longer than large ones, sometimes reaching 16–18 years or even more, whereas giant breeds are considered pensioners at the age of only eight or nine years. Large dogs, such as Labradors and Golden Retrievers, tend to live for an average of 13–14 years.

Whatever your dog's age, make sure his quality of life is top notch by giving him the best in food, exercise and mental stimulation.

understanding
canine language

talk the talk

Learning to 'read' your dog means that you can communicate with her and keep her safe. You will be able to address her emotional and physical needs and be sympathetic to her moods. It's essential to be able to spot stress in your dog – city living is difficult enough, but not being understood could make life almost unbearable, so learn to 'talk the talk'.

Learning your dog's language

You will already have realized that dog language is subtle and complex. Even though dogs don't talk, they have many different ways of communicating their emotions and their intentions to each other and to us.

Learning 'canine' as a second language is important if you are to avoid misinterpretations and the clash of cultures that can result – especially with the cosmopolitan canine; you need to address any stress that your dog experiences before it becomes critical, for the sake both of her well-being and of your relationship with her.

Dogs watch human beings constantly. They are masters at predicting our actions, our routines and even our moods. Indeed, some dogs can even learn to predict when we are going out, or when visitors are about to arrive. This is not some sixth sense, but the ability to detect tiny changes in our behaviour that tell the dog something is about to happen. Dogs are so good at doing this that some are even trained to detect when a person is going to have an epileptic seizure – they can predict this up to an hour before it is going to happen, giving the epileptic person time to seek medical help.

Mixed signals

All dogs use eye contact to communicate with one another – and with humans. Direct head-on staring is a little threatening to dogs (and to humans; we too feel uncomfortable if someone stares at us). For this reason, some dogs don't like to look directly at their owners; instead, they are being polite by looking away, although 'old-school' dog trainers often misinterpret this, claiming that the dog is being disobedient.

Just as we have to learn the meaning of our dogs' postures and signals, so dogs have to learn what humans mean by their words and gestures. This happens very early on, during the socialization period, when they discover that humans show their teeth when they smile, but are not being aggressive; and that we may make loud noises, such as sneezing or laughing, which are no threat.

Sadly, miscommunications between dogs and people can result in misery, trauma or even aggression. Dogs that are wagging their tails are not always happy – indeed, this can indicate uncertainty just before a dog decides to bite. People may also mistake canine expressions of fear as a dog showing guilt (a purely human emotion), which can lead an owner to believe that their dog knows she has done wrong and should not behave that way again.

The physical characteristics of some breeds can make reading their facial expressions more challenging both for you and for other dogs.

Global understanding

Dogs of different breeds all seem to speak the same language, although their physical make-up may create problems on occasions. For example, breeds with docked tails or cropped ears may find it more difficult to signal their intentions, as their physical changes clearly limit their communication abilities. Dogs with upright ears or tails may inadvertently look as if they are being threatening towards other dogs, when their intentions are purely peaceful. Interestingly, canine language also seems to be consistent throughout the world – a dog living in Tokyo is able to understand a canine cousin from Paris with no problem at all.

in the mood

Those who live with dogs know that animals have moods that can be influenced by the environment, which can in turn affect the way dogs behave. Imagine trying to train a German Shepherd Dog not to bark at the front door when she has not been exercised for several days. Clearly, her emotional state will affect her ability to concentrate, learn and control her own impulses.

Such aspects of emotionality may seem obvious, but some researchers think we can take the subject even further. Of course, this presents a problem: how can we talk about animal emotions without attributing human beliefs, values and judgements to them? The answers are not as simple as they may at first appear, but hesitant initial steps towards exploring animal behaviour are now being made. In the meantime, it is important that we look at well-founded evidence and at information such as body language and observable behaviour to try and determine exactly how our dogs are feeling.

What makes your dog happy?

Physical activity goes hand in hand with pleasure for many dogs. For instance, a Jack Russell Terrier is likely to enjoy running – just for the sake of it; and bouncing up and down may also come into her repertoire of fun things to do. Such activity may be an expression of pleasure or may induce it. For this reason alone, dogs need exercise. Large, active dogs obviously need more physical activity than lapdogs, but all canines benefit from the freedom and fitness that exercise can bring.

More specifically, what makes your dog happy will often depend on what she has been bred to do. For example, herding dogs love to chase, gundogs to retrieve items, terriers to dig and hounds to track scents. If you own a cross-breed or mongrel, look at the type that your dog represents – is she more like a hound or a herder? (See pages 16–19 for more information about breed characteristics.)

Creating urban alternatives

Unfortunately, many of the behaviours that our dogs love to perform are inappropriate in a city setting. For instance, chasing and herding are pretty much off the cards in town, unless you create suitable scenarios in the park where your dog can perform these activities, but in a controlled way. Teaching your dog to run after and catch a Frisbee™ can be an outlet for chasing and rounding up, as well as for retrieving – with the added bonus that your dog cannot catch the Frisbee™ and bark at the same time!

We need to ensure that our urban dogs get the opportunity to perform natural, rewarding behaviour in a way that enhances our lives too, and to do this we have to recognize their emotional states so that we can tell what makes them happy.

Love me

Most dogs love affection and enjoy being stroked and touched, particularly on the chest and rump. They may ask for this attention by approaching someone and resting their head against them, looking up at them with soft, squinty eyes. However, many dogs do not appreciate being patted on the head, and this is something they may have to learn to tolerate in urban environments, where strangers often approach and touch dogs without asking their owners first.

To help your dog cope with this, it is a good idea to pair food treats occasionally with touching her on the head and back – in this way she will always make positive associations with the feel of human hands. You can even make this into a training game so that your dog comes to expect that touch equals treat, especially from children.

The type of attention your dog enjoys will be individual. Some love to be touched and stroked; others prefer praise and games. Watch her reaction to see which she favours.

language lessons

Learning canine as a foreign language takes time and patience on your part, but keep watching your dog and you will begin to see a whole gamut of subtle signals and expressions that other dog owners barely notice. These will improve your communication with your pet and will deepen your relationship with her.

Play bow

In the play bow – perhaps the most obvious of the play signals – the dog dips her head and chest to the floor, keeping the elbows on the ground, while leaving the bottom and tail high in the air. This is often accompanied by a 'play face' whereby the dog draws back her lips and turns her face to one side. This play signal is often misinterpreted by owners, who think their dog is trying to attack them! This is perhaps understandable, for the signal probably originates in the practice of predatory sequences: both puppies and adult dogs assume this posture in an attempt to start a chase game, which would later be used for hunting expertise.

Paw raise

This simple gesture has its roots in the dog's early puppyhood. Newborn pups knead their mother's belly to stimulate milk production while feeding, and this gradually becomes a pacifying gesture. However, many dogs learn to use this signal to their own advantage, usually to gain attention when they want it. Hundreds of jogged coffee cups attest to the power of this action! Many dogs also use paw raises to indicate play intention with other dogs.

Taken one step further, a heavy paw can be used to hold another dog down, and to indicate challenge if it is placed on the other dog's shoulders. Some adult dogs use one heavy paw to gently restrain aberrant puppies – and literally hold them at arm's length.

Jump up

Perhaps the most problematic of the obvious body postures, jumping up often signals friendliness – the dog is attempting to get as close as possible to a human's face, to lick or make indirect eye contact. This action is learned during puppyhood, when pups attempt to solicit food from adults' mouth by licking around their lips. Of course, if they try the same behaviour with us, they are forced to jump up to our height to do so.

However, jumping up takes several forms. Dogs that jump up to gain affection and be sociable nearly always do so with a 'soft' approach. Even though they may be heavy and cumbersome, the jumping is usually 'squirmy' and wriggly, rather than direct and forceful. The other form of jumping up indicates more of a 'testing' approach, whereby a dog uses her body weight to bounce off the human, rather than attempting to make friendly contact. Such dogs are often feeling over-excited or stressed, rather than purely sociable.

Hip swing

Hip swings or nudges are often seen during canine play. The real experts at this are German Shepherd Dogs, which seem to love swinging round and knocking other dogs gently (or not so gently) with their rear ends. This is an obvious play signal, for the rear end is clearly safe: the playmates are saying, 'Look, no teeth here.'

Dogs also present their rear ends to humans for attention. The intention varies with the type of dog and the situation in which it occurs. For example, some dogs will present their rear ends for a scratch, to indicate that they mean no harm and to show that they trust you. Other dogs, however, may be saying, 'You have permission to scratch my butt!' – but will walk away when they have had enough.

On the whole dogs jump up as a friendly gesture, in order to solicit our attention. However, it is annoying for us! See pages 108–109 for help with Jumping Up.

Yawning

Human beings yawn for several different reasons: to gain more oxygen, to indicate stress, through embarrassment or sheer boredom. Dogs also yawn for different reasons, and the meaning can depend on the context. Interestingly, yawning seems to be just as 'contagious' among dogs as it is among humans. Yawning in front of your dog may result in several different responses: she may assume that you are under stress and turn or move away from you. Equally, she may yawn in response. Dogs and other species resting together will often be triggered into a yawning 'wave', when one starts off and the others follow.

Dogs that yawn during training or when meeting people in the city may be showing that they feel confused or slightly threatened in some way. If your dog demonstrates this behaviour in training, or when you are out and about, the time has come to review your methods or to ask why she may be experiencing stress – it may be that she needs more confidence in social situations.

Licking

Lip licking is often seen in combination with yawning when a dog feels herself under pressure or facing a threat. Like paw raising, it originates in neonatal behaviour during suckling and, later, in attempting to solicit food by licking around the mouths of other adult dogs. Puppies often show this behaviour when they meet adult dogs, especially if they feel insecure. Occasionally puppies continue this action into adolescence and will lick their owners or other dogs excessively – to the infuriation of both.

Later in life, licking can also be regarded as a part of sexual behaviour. Some dogs, particularly entire males, find odour-stained patches of grass, carpet or another dog's genitals almost impossible to resist, and may drool and chatter their teeth as they lick up the chemical signals. This behaviour enables the dog to analyse the information fully using their Jacobson's organ: a special organ situated in the roof of the mouth that enables the dog to taste and smell chemical particles simultaneously.

Rolling over

Think of a dog rolling over, and most owners will imagine that the dog is hoping to have her tummy rubbed, or they will imagine that she is being submissive or appeasing. This may be so, but dogs also use rolling over to demonstrate passive resistance. Frequently seen in gundogs, this is an attempt to prevent a threat or action by resisting in a defensive, but indirect way. Perhaps the most common example occurs during a veterinary examination or when an owner tries to clip a dog's nails. The dog resists by throwing herself onto her back and using her feet to push the owner away. If this fails, she may use inhibited mouthing to prevent the owner's actions. The dog may look cute and playful during this encounter, and may use another play strategy as soon as possible after getting up, to deflect her owner's behaviour.

Appeasement urination

Even after becoming house-trained, some dogs may continue to leak a little urine when they first meet someone new or greet family members as they come home. This can of course be particularly embarrassing if you are out and about, meeting people socially in the hub of a town or city. On the whole, young dogs do grow out of this behaviour as their confidence in the environment increases and they mature physically. But occasionally it is caused by overbearing greetings from people who don't realize they are frightening the dog. Encouraging people to greet your dog sideways on, avoiding direct eye contact and perhaps offering a food treat as a greeting gesture, can help enormously.

Often misinterpreted as 'submission', this dog is pushing her owner away in a show of passive resistance.

mind your language!

Given that people who speak the same language still manage to misunderstand each other, the aim of enjoying straightforward communication with our dogs is a challenging one. Many common canine behavioural problems are the result of misinterpretations between humans and dogs, so the more we know about our differences and our similarities, the better.

Tail wagging

Tail wagging means that a dog is happy and friendly, doesn't it? Unfortunately, this is not always so. The position of the tail, how fast it is wagging and in what context reveal a great deal about a dog's intentions – and they are not always positive.

Tail positions depend on physical construction, but dogs that hold their tails right up are usually indicating confidence, assertive behaviour or high excitement. Dogs with tails held in neutral – that is, level with the body or slightly lower – are usually feeling relaxed, friendly and secure. A tail that is held low, or even between the legs, is generally indicative of anxiety, uncertainty or fear. Sadly, many dog aggression victims report that the dog was wagging its tail when it bit them; the dog was not enjoying being aggressive – it was indicating uncertainty about the situation.

Hugs and cuddles

Part of the reason why many of us keep dogs is that we want to have close physical contact with them. However, our dogs may not always understand what is happening when we try to cuddle them, especially if they have not learned that this is a human way of being friendly. Puppies in particular may not want to be held close or tightly, and may object by wriggling, squealing or biting.

Divided by a common language! This little girl is enjoying a hug, but her dog is not. For safety reasons, children should always keep their faces away from dogs' faces.

In a wild environment, physical restraint would probably mean one of two things to a puppy: either a predator had hold of it or it was being mounted – neither of which is terribly desirable and both of which necessitate defence and a quick escape. Many domestic dogs learn that such human contact is pleasurable, but it does take time.

first-night
nerves

making your home puppy-proof

You are planning to go and get your puppy. The whole family is excited – but do remember that a few preparations now will save a great deal of stress later on. Your pup's safety is of paramount importance. Bear in mind that puppies will eat and chew almost anything, so put out of his reach anything that could harm your puppy and make sure you have a safe area ready and waiting.

Safety first

Have a look around your home and try to see the environment from a puppy's-eye-view. Go from room to room and look especially for items that he might eat or chew, or anything that might cause injury as a result of falling on him. Puppies have no sense of hazard or danger from traffic and height – particular concerns in an urban environment – or even from heat, so you need to think for him in the early days.

Kitchen

Your kitchen is likely to be the centre of your pup's world. It's a great place for him, as it's the heart of the household and is easily cleaned. But remember that low cupboards may contain household detergents, cleaners or chemicals that could harm your puppy, and that trailing cables can be fatal if chewed. Some seemingly innocent foodstuffs are also toxic to dogs – surprisingly, chocolate, onions and even raisins can be harmful.

Living room

Rugs, cushions and remote-control devices are all favourite chew toys for puppies. Some house plants,

On a mission! Puppies love to explore, so you need to make sure that their environment is safe and always supervise your dog's antics.

Balcony and stairs

Puppies have very little awareness of height risks – they can easily fall down stairs or from balconies – and in the city, where many people live in apartments, this is a special danger. Indeed, even an open window can lure a puppy to look over the edge. Use a baby gate or fly screen to prevent your dog escaping into the street or falling from a height.

Garden and garage

Your garden or back yard can offer hours of fun for your puppy, but also hazards from poisonous plants, insects and chemicals stored in sheds or garages. Puppies should not be left unsupervised in these areas, for they inevitably get into trouble by chewing unsuitable items. Ponds and swimming pools can be particularly dangerous, because once in the water puppies tire quickly and cannot get out.

such as ferns and umbrella plants (*Schefflera arboricola*), can be poisonous, so put them up out of reach for the time being.

Bathroom

Beware the contents of your bathroom cupboard! Nearly all prescription drugs and many other tablets, such as painkillers and cough lozenges, can be fatal to dogs, even in small doses.

Bedroom

Watch out for cables, as well as make-up and beauty products. Many dogs seem attracted to playing with dirty laundry, and vets frequently have to surgically remove socks that puppies have swallowed. Children's bedrooms can be particularly risky, because small plastic toys and items such as rubber bands, pens and hair scrunchies seem irresistible to puppies and are often found at floor level.

Making time

It's important that you spend time with your new puppy when you first bring him home, in order to bond with him, help him settle and start good house-training habits. If possible, take a few days off work to do this, but remember that during this time you must also teach your pup to be alone for short periods. Allowing him continual access to you may create over-bonding, which will become a problem when you go back to work in the city.

Putting your pup in a dog crate or indoor kennel (see pages 42–43), or behind a baby gate in one room while you potter about in another, is a good way of starting to teach him that it's just part of his daily routine to be left alone.

the homecoming

All puppies are different – some come bounding into their new urban home oozing confidence, while others take a little longer to feel secure. However, don't be fooled. What may look like bravery at home may not be transferred to the big city at large, so make sure you take the time to settle your pup in and build his confidence, no matter what his initial attitude.

Gaining confidence

For most puppies, leaving their mother and littermates is a dramatic change, and this will be compounded if they have come to the city from a rural area that has been much quieter. Make the first day at home a gentle affair, allowing the pup to become familiar with you, your home and your family. Be careful that he is not overwhelmed by the attentions of children – their friends can come and see him once he has settled in for a couple of days.

Don't expect too much of your puppy on the first day. He may have been practically house-trained while still with his breeder, but much of what a puppy learns is context-specific, so it may take a bit of time for him to transfer his understanding to his new environment (see pages 46–47).

Elders and betters

If you already have an older dog, keep in mind that first impressions really do count. It can be a good idea to take him with you when you fetch the new puppy, if that is practical. Meeting on neutral territory fosters acceptance between the two dogs and prevents territory-guarding by your older dog, which may see the newcomer as a threat to the home or family.

Once back home, ensure that the two dogs are supervised together and that the pup does not pester the older dog too much. If he does, and the older dog won't tell him off, this simply tells your puppy it is acceptable behaviour with all other dogs – and it is going to get him into trouble in the park before he's too much older. If your existing dog can't or won't discipline the new puppy appropriately, you must step in and break up the action. Such intervention needs to be frequent and consistent. There is no need for punishment – just halt the fun by saying 'finish', then distracting the dogs with a toy or chew, or by putting the pup in a dog crate or behind a baby gate for a few moments to calm down.

Interestingly, it seems that a puppy coming into a home where an older dog already exists needs *more* socialization with other dogs, not less, or he will become over-attached to the older dog and more fearful of unknown animals. But he needs to do this on his own, without his new friend there to back him up. This means getting him out and about to meet and mix with other dogs on separate walks and city excursions as often as possible. Your pup will never learn to stand on his own four paws unless you invest time in him individually now.

Other animals

Introductions to cats and other pets – whether your own or someone else's – need to be carefully planned to ensure they go smoothly. In a city environment, where you probably live in close proximity to your neighbours and their animals, it's quite a good idea to introduce them to your pet.

It's essential that cats are able to escape up onto high surfaces to get away from a new puppy, without

Most adult dogs are gentle with new puppies, but it is sensible to arrange for the first meeting between your puppy and your other dog to be on neutral territory if you can.

being chased. Keep your cat in a travelling basket, or use a physical barrier such as a baby gate, to make the first few moments of the meeting safe and trauma-free. If your pup shows no interest in the cat, praise him and give him a treat to reward the right behaviour. If he shows an inclination to chase, prevent this by keeping him on a lead, and do brief introductions often, under careful supervision.

More than one

Owning more than one dog is double the pleasure, but also twice the commitment. Your puppy will need a great deal of time with you, playing and being trained independently of his older friend. He will also need to be taken out alone to develop good social skills. However, make sure you continue to give your older dog walks, training and plenty of attention to prevent sibling rivalry.

your first night together

Your puppy has come from the security of his mother and littermates, and his first night away from all the familiar sounds and smells may well cause him some anxiety. This can result in crying, whining and barking. There is much you can do to make him feel more comfortable, but don't forget that bad habits are hard to break. Here are some dos and don'ts.

Dos

✳ **Bed rest** Do make sure your dog has a comfy, cosy bed of his own. This does not have to be fancy or expensive, but does need to be tucked out of the way of the main traffic in your home. Puppies need a lot of sleep in their first few weeks – just like human babies – and can become irritable if they are deprived of it. A dog crate or indoor kennel (see pages 42–43) is ideal, because it offers 360-degree protection and will become a haven for your dog from fast-paced city living, once he has been properly introduced to it.

✳ **Comfort stop** Do check that your puppy has been out to the toilet before bed. Many pups can be quite distracted by the overwhelming array of sights and sounds in their new home and, even when taken outside, can forget what they are there for. Be patient and make sure he is comfortable before you settle him down for the night. Puppies have small bladders and little control – and small breeds have even less capacity to wait to go to the toilet than bigger dogs. Be prepared to get up in the night to take your puppy outside – or, at the very least, to get up early. Puppy pads – flat pads that absorb urine and are placed on the floor, like a litter tray – are now available. They can assist in house-training if you live in a city apartment or don't have speedy access to the outdoors; however, be judicious about their use, and phase them out as soon as you can to avoid dependency.

✳ **Mini-separations** Do practise 'sleeping arrangements' during the day. This may sound a little odd, but puppies often fail to sleep well on their first few nights in a new home because their sleeping area is unfamiliar to them. To prevent this, every time your puppy looks sleepy during the day, pick him up and place him in the area where you want him to sleep at night. Then leave him there in peace. If he whines, cries or barks ignore him until he falls asleep.

* **Visual contact** Do accept that it is okay to place your puppy's bed or crate in the bedroom with you – or at least somewhere close so that you can maintain visual or vocal contact. After all, dogs are social animals and suffer greatly when they feel isolated, especially on the first night in a new home. If you do not wish to have your dog in the bedroom or close by when he's an adult, gradually move his bed or crate further away over a period of a few nights or weeks, until you are happy with the final destination.

Don'ts

* **Bed sharing** Don't be tempted to take your new puppy into bed with you, or allow your children to have the puppy in bed with them. Although it may be fun for the first few nights, your puppy will come to depend on the close contact and will expect this to happen forever.

* **Punishment** Don't shout at or be cross with your puppy if he is keeping you awake by barking, howling or whining. His behaviour will be the result of feeling insecure, and any apparent aggression from you will only serve to make it worse. Instead, settle him back down again with minimum fuss, then ignore him until he falls asleep.

Puppies rely on their mother and littermates for comfort and security, so be patient and understanding in the first days and nights with you but away from them.

crate training, step by step

Teaching your dog to stay in an indoor kennel, or crate, can be a wonderful way of protecting your home and keeping your dog safe and secure at the same time. When introduced properly, an indoor kennel is not a cage in which to keep your pet incarcerated, but a cosy bed and a welcome refuge from the hectic urban world.

Crate training is perfect for city puppies and for newly rehomed dogs. Dogs rarely soil their own bed area, so using a crate as your dog's bed can greatly assist with speedy and stress-free house-training. Many crates are designed to pack flat when not in use, making them great for travelling or for general use in the city home during particularly busy periods. They can then be stored out of the way when not in use.

What size?

The crate should give your dog enough room to lie down comfortably and stretch out. He should be able to sit or stand up without bumping his head, and be able to turn round easily. Some people decide to use a crate for their adult dog too, while others dispense with them as soon as their pup is house-trained, so the size of crate you purchase will depend on this.

Preparing the crate

The crate should look and feel like a comfortable nest – not a barren plastic or metal cage. Place plenty of soft bedding (old towels and blankets will do) inside it. Do not use newspaper or your pup may associate the crate with toileting. Provide a range of chews and toys in the crate for amusement. You will also need a non-spill water bowl – this can be attached to the side of the crate with clips to ensure that it stays put.

Positive associations

Never use the crate as a punishment area. If your dog needs 'time out', use a baby gate or exclude him from your company. The crate should always be associated with comfort and security.

Teaching use of the crate

Place the crate in a family location, where your puppy can be involved with the rest of the household, but where he is out of the main bustle and traffic. Isolating your puppy in another room while you are all in the living room will only cause frustration, and your dog will be unlikely to settle. Ensure children are aware that the crate is not a playhouse and that they should not disturb the dog while he is in there.

1 Let your dog explore the crate on his own. Do not force him in, but build pleasant associations by feeding him in there and by throwing in treats and chew toys. Leave the door open at all times to start with.

2 Once he is confident about entering the crate, move on to the next stage. Make up his dinner and, with lots of encouragement, place the bowl inside and shut the door – with your dog on the outside! Let your dog get a little frustrated at being able to see and smell his dinner, but not get to it, then open the crate door and let him in. Close the door behind him, but only while he is eating. Open it again as soon as he has finished and take him outside to the toilet.

3 Repeat this process until your dog just loves going into the crate – indeed, a good sign is when you find him in there, looking hopeful! At this stage you can extend the amount of time your dog spends sleeping and eating in the crate. Apart from sleeping in it overnight, the maximum a puppy should be left in a crate is two hours. Always make sure he has plenty of drinking water and fun things to chew. Before your dog goes in the crate, check that he has had some exercise and a chance to relieve himself, and always spend quality time with him afterwards.

handle with care

All dogs need to get used to being handled – and should learn to associate it with pleasure and security, not confrontation and discomfort. Indeed, they should regard the approach of human hands as loving and enjoyable. Never punish your puppy by smacking or hitting him. Even a 'tap on the nose' can make a dog hand-shy for life.

Handling is very different from simply stroking or cuddling. Handling prepares your dog for examination at the veterinary surgery, for grooming, nail clipping and being given medical treatment. In order to build your dog's confidence when being handled, it is a good idea to make it a daily occurrence.

Checking ears, mouth and paws

Stand your puppy on a non-slip surface, and have some tasty food treats to hand. Check him all over, starting with his ears, by lifting the flaps and having a good look inside. The ear should look pink and clean, and should be free of any discharge or odour that could indicate infection.

Look at your pup's mouth, too. Lift the lips on one side, then the other, pushing the puppy's lip up from underneath, rather than putting your whole hand over the top of his muzzle, because many dogs object to this. Dogs lose their deciduous or puppy teeth at

To check your puppy's teeth, push his lip up from below rather than placing your whole hand over his muzzle.

around 16–20 weeks, so see if you can spot any missing puppy teeth.

Pick up each paw in turn and gently push your fingers between the pads. This enables you to check for any foreign bodies such as grass seeds, which can work their way into the skin. Check that his nails are not over-long. Many dogs seem to have sensitive feet and tails, so be patient and reward your puppy with treats for calm, quiet behaviour.

Veterinary matters

Make sure you register with a veterinary surgeon as soon as you get your puppy. Your city practice will be able to advise you on all the necessary vaccinations for urban living, and on preventative healthcare to ensure that your dog has a long and healthy life.

the good-
behaviour guide

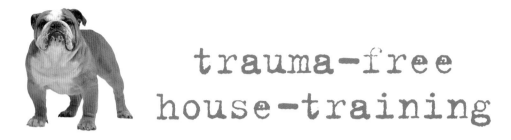

trauma-free house-training

The basics of house-training are very simple, at least in principle: never let your puppy go in the wrong place – and praise and reward her when she gets it right. Don't feel guilty if you live in a city apartment; house-training might take a little longer at first, but your efforts in taking her out frequently will mean that you can guarantee reliability in the long term.

House-training guidelines

House-training is largely a matter of establishing a rigorous routine and following the same procedure until your puppy has learned all the principles.

* Take your pup outside on the hour, every hour, during the day and evening. This is particularly important if you live in an urban apartment, because you do not want to wait until your pup is desperate to relieve herself before venturing outside. Wait with her until she goes to the toilet, then praise her profusely.

* Repeat the process after your puppy has woken up, after she has eaten and after an exciting event, such as the children coming home from school. Your puppy will usually start to sniff around and turn in circles when she is about to go to the toilet. Quickly encourage her to follow you outside if you have a yard or garden, or to the puppy

pad (see page 40) if you are using one indoors. If you live in an apartment and your puppy is a little older, encourage her to walk towards the door, then attach her lead and take her outside. As soon as she goes in the right place, praise her quietly and reward her with a food treat.

✱ If your puppy doesn't go to the toilet after about five minutes, take her back indoors or to another area and supervise her carefully, before trying again 15 minutes later. This means not taking your eyes off her for a second!

✱ If she has an accident, clean it up calmly, using biological detergent solution if appropriate. Do not scold your puppy, even if you catch her in the act, as this will make her wary of going to the toilet in your presence. Punishment of any kind may simply delay house-training and harm your relationship with your dog. Make sure your puppy learns by trial and success.

✱ Some puppies take longer than others to have full control through the night. After about 14 weeks it is fair to expect that most can manage this. Make sure your puppy has been to the toilet before bed, then confine her to a small area, such as an indoor crate.

It is quite unusual for dogs to soil their own bed area, so get your vet to check her over if she does, to ensure she is healthy.

Toileting on command

It can be useful to give your pup a command to go to the toilet. Simply choose a command that is suitable, such as 'Be quick'; then, each time she goes to the toilet, say your command while she is going and reward her afterwards. After a short period your pup will associate the command with going to the toilet outside, and this will automatically stimulate her to go to the toilet on cue. Use the following guidelines:

✱ Praise and reward her when she goes in the right place.
✱ Be consistent in supervising your puppy for a whole weekend, and you will be pleased and surprised at how quickly she can be clean.
✱ If you can't keep an eye on her, restrict her to a crate or to an easily cleaned area.
✱ Avoid punishment. Even scolding can be enough to create anxiety in a sensitive pup and can delay effective house-training.

Puppy pads are a relatively new invention for pet owners. Like a flat nappy, they can assist in house-training and can save your carpets at the outset.

house rules to live by

There is little doubt that prevention is better than cure. This means that although puppies come fully equipped with huge, adoring eyes and appealing faces, you must resist giving in to their every whim! Living in the city offers many delights, but also certain constraints, and putting boundaries in place for your dog now will save you stress and time later on.

Play biting

It comes as a huge shock to most new puppy owners that their little bundle of fluff comes armed with a set of teeth that a shark would be proud of! Your dog's deciduous or puppy teeth are as sharp as needles, and are designed to hurt. Puppies under the age of about 18 weeks use their mouths just as toddlers do: to explore the world and discover what is alive and what is not. For this reason, they want to put anything and everything – including your hands and skin – into their mouths. Your puppy will also bite in play, just as she would with her littermates. This is completely normal and should not be treated as aggression. However, it is not acceptable for dogs to bite people – and puppies need to learn how to moderate their biting before they lose their puppy teeth at around 18 weeks of age.

How to control puppy biting

Your puppy needs to know that biting hurts – not that you are angry or that it gains attention. This means that each and every time your puppy mouths your hands or clothes, you need to:

* Yelp loudly or give a loud 'Ouch!'
* Immediately turn away.
* Ignore your pup for about 20 seconds, then resume interacting with her.
* Repeat the 'Ouch!' and turn away *every* time you feel her teeth.

This procedure needs to be carried out consistently by everyone in the household. Biting will not stop immediately. Instead, it should become less and less hard over a period of three to four weeks. By this point your pup should realize that she cannot put any pressure on you at all – finally teaching her that she cannot initiate biting in any circumstances.

Puppy biting is a normal part of canine behaviour, but it does need to be modified for safety.

Your pup is what she eats

If your puppy is very excitable or over-active, you may need to have a look at her diet. We now know that what puppies are fed can directly affect their behaviour and learning ability. However, this can be difficult to spot. If your dog is going to the toilet a lot, eating unusual things such as tissues, or seems to be irritable or short-tempered, it may be worth trying a change of diet. Results can often be seen in days so it is well worth asking your veterinary surgeon for advice.

Teaching your pup like this is an essential part of city living. It is unacceptable for dogs to approach people and put their mouths on them, no matter how friendly and sociable the dog really is. This is particularly the case with children, who may become frightened by the behaviour and whose reactions can then fuel the dog to further excitement.

Wrestling games

One of the activities that can create many behavioural problems in later life is playing rough games with your puppy. This teaches your pup that it is acceptable for her to put her teeth on human clothes, skin and hair, and is simply brewing up trouble for later on. For this reason never allow your pup to play wrestling games with kids or adults – use a toy such as a ragger (cotton-blend rope) toy instead, or play training games that will teach your pup good manners for life.

polite society

For a perfect start to your puppy's life with you, it is essential to establish rules from the very beginning. Some of these rules are particularly important for urban life, because a well-mannered dog will be able to enjoy far more freedom out and about in the city than one that becomes a public liability.

Greeting behaviour

Teaching your dog to sit politely to greet visitors or passers-by in the street can be a real winner. You will be surprised at just how many people stop to say hello to your puppy when she's out and about, but there's nothing more annoying or embarrassing than having her leap all over them in great excitement – especially when she's a year old and can reach their shoulders with her paws!

Bear in mind that asking your puppy to sit is simple, and is easily rewarded. However, this behaviour does not come naturally, so you will have to work at it until it is perfect. Start with family and friends: every time your pup greets them, ask her to sit, then praise her, pet her and give her a food treat for complying. Practise this until the behaviour is automatic. You can then introduce more 'unusual' greetings by getting your puppy to sit and stay (see pages 76–77) while you clap your hands, jump up and down, and wave your hands in the air. This is useful because children may greet your puppy in a far more excitable fashion than adults. They may well leap up and down, wave their arms and squeal with excitement! Your dog needs to have been trained to cope with this before it happens in the street.

Say no to titbits

Never, ever feed your pup titbits from the table or from snacks that you are eating. Even doing this randomly will encourage her to beg and it can lead to stealing and mugging, where the dog snatches food from children or even from strangers!

Table manners

Just imagine yourself sitting in an open-air café, meeting friends and enjoying a coffee with your faithful hound at your feet. Now imagine the same dog bounding about, knocking cups and tables flying, barking and lungeing, or trying to steal food from your friends' plates. There is no doubt that table manners matter! To train perfect behaviour at human mealtimes, use the following steps.

1 At least to start with, ensure that everyone is sitting up at the table to eat. It is almost impossible to train a puppy to ignore food if children are sitting on the floor – with food at nose height. Also, provide a 'settle-down' area where your dog is expected to rest while the family is eating. This could be her bed, a crate or just a mat on the floor.

2 Take your puppy to the mat or bed and ask her to settle down on it. Encourage her to do so with a food treat if necessary (see pages 78–79). Then immediately give her a chew or a toy stuffed with food that will keep her occupied for the duration of your meal.

3 If your puppy gets up and comes to the table, quietly take her back and settle her down again. Be thoroughly consistent and you will soon find that the words 'Settle down' will prompt your pup to go to her special area and lie down patiently. You can then use this command at other times as well, giving her a chance to take time out, if urban life gets too hectic.

preventing chewing and barking

All puppies need to chew! This is natural behaviour and brings pleasure, as it soothes teething pain and provides entertainment. However, a pup's view of what is good to chew does not necessarily match ours. Puppies will 'test' almost anything for texture, taste and 'chewability' – and if they discover a predilection for your hallway carpet, it can become a habit for life.

It's all chewable to pups

Providing an abundance of chew toys is vitally important if you are to direct your puppy's innate desire to chew onto appropriate items. One or two rather boring plastic toys are simply not good enough. Although your home may resemble a nursery school for a few weeks, it is definitely worth putting up with this to prevent valuable items being sacrificed. Have a think about what your puppy would like to chew, rather than what you think she *ought* to chew. Many toys sold in pet shops can be destroyed in seconds, and those with squeakers in them are potentially dangerous if they are swallowed. Pig's ears and cooked bones often cause digestive upsets, while very hard items can break a dog's teeth.

Some of the best chew toys are Nylabones™ (chewable 'bones' made from natural nylon) and Kongs (hollow rubber pyramids that can be filled with

Separation anxiety

If your dog barks or howls when you leave her home alone, it is possible that she is suffering from a separation-related disorder and is expressing her distress or frustration at being left. Check out the advice given on pages 136–137.

Barking and howling are a natural part of canine vocal communication and many dogs (if not their human owners) really enjoy it.

delicious bits of food, which fall out as the pup chews – thus neatly rewarding the dog for chewing the right thing, see pages 130–131). These are perfect for leaving with your dog when you have to go out or when she needs to entertain herself. You can even find on the Internet recipes featuring various ingredients for 'Kong stuffing'.

If you have provided lots of engaging toys and chews and your dog is still chewing – particularly when you go out – it may be that she is experiencing some anxiety about being separated from you. If you suspect this is the case, contact your veterinary practice for advice and follow the guidelines on pages 136–137.

Peace and quiet

There are many reasons why dogs bark. Barking is, of course, an integral part of normal canine behaviour, and as such dogs can be expressing loneliness, frustration, boredom, anxiety, fear and aggression. Dogs also bark when they are playing, excited or just letting off steam. Some breeds bark more than others, often because this is what they were originally bred to do – and this nearly always needs redirection rather than an attempt to 'cure' it. However, in an urban environment, barking can be distinctly antisocial, and for the sake of good neighbourly relations it needs to be prevented.

All dogs can also learn to bark for attention and this is certainly preventable. All that is required is an understanding by you that what gets rewarded gets repeated. This means that if your puppy sits by the biscuit cupboard and barks, and you laugh, get up and give her a biscuit, it's very likely she will do it again! Have a think about what rewards your dog might be getting for barking, if you already have the hint of a problem. Shouting at your dog must seem like barking encouragement; giving eye contact or chasing her, the equivalent of a doggie lottery win!

Overall, the simplest way to prevent barking from becoming a problem is to keep your dog occupied, and to ignore barking whenever possible to prevent it from being inadvertently rewarded. In our cheek-by-jowl urban environment, it is essential never to let it become a habit.

keeping ownership of your furniture

One of the main complaints owners have is that their once-cute puppy turns into a huge, hairy beast that takes possession of their furniture. If you don't want your dog on the furniture, make a rule and stick to it. Don't be tempted to allow your puppy up, even for the occasional cuddle, or she'll discover what she's missing and it will start the habit of a lifetime.

Sofa squabbles

Of course dogs want to get on the furniture. This has nothing to do with 'dominance', but is simply because furniture is comfortable and smells like us. Whether you want your pet to get on your sofa is a personal decision, but if you own a large dog or one that sheds a lot of hair, it is always best to think ahead. Do you really want her climbing up next to visitors wearing smart clothing, or clambering on next door's children when they come to visit?

If you find that your dog is keen to discover the delights of your armchairs when she's left on her own, either block access to them by placing items on the cushions or keep her out of the room in question altogether.

If you choose to allow your dog on the furniture, then it's perfectly reasonable to let her lie on certain pieces and not on others – as long as you are consistent in your approach, this can work well. Placing a throw over the sofa that your dog is allowed on and inviting her up teaches her that this place is permitted, but you must be consistent about preventing access to the other furniture at all times.

Duvet dramas

Your bed is a prized area – and what dog wouldn't want to make herself comfortable in the middle of the duvet? Once again, whether to allow your dog on the bed is a matter of personal choice, but it's wise to bear in mind that some dogs – especially small ones – can start to become possessive over the area as adolescents, and that preventing a behavioural problem is always easier than curing one, so start training early by rewarding her for jumping off when asked.

Doorway control

Teaching doorway control is easy. For simple safety reasons, your dog should not barge past you when you open a door – especially in the city, where traffic flows freely and life is unpredictable. Polite manners at doorways will also make urban life easier for you and will give your heelwork training a head start (see pages 84–85). Dogs learn this exercise really fast – they understand that the door only opens when they take a step backwards, and that it closes in front of them if they try to push through. Make sure you practise at different doorways to establish the behaviour, no matter where you are. You can also use this technique to train your cosmopolitan canine not to jump out of the car (see pages 96–97).

1 With your dog on a lead, take her towards the door. Open the door only a crack. If your dog goes to push her nose through, close the door – being careful not to shut her nose in it! Repeat immediately.

2 Most dogs need to repeat this exercise four to six times before they get the hint and take a step *backwards* or move to the side, whenever the door is opened.

3 You can now open the door wider and wider until it is fully open, but your dog is not showing any interest in going through. At this point, you can invite her to step through the door with you – practise makes perfect.

communal living

Living in the city often necessitates close contact with other people and dogs. Ironically, this has major advantages for dogs, because their encounters with unfamiliar people provide above-average socialization in their early weeks – vital for a confident attitude later in life. However, such interactions with neighbours and other city dwellers mean that they need to learn social etiquette early on.

Going up

When travelling in lifts, all dogs should be carried or taught to sit or stand still next to their owner. On occasions when lifts are crowded, teaching your dog to stand behind you, next to the back or side wall, can be an advantage as it keeps paws and tail away from pushchair wheels, feet and the hazards of automatic doors.

However, even if you generally use the lift in your apartment building, it is a good idea to familiarize your dog with going up and down stairs, because this is essential for use in an emergency.

Balconies, yards and hallways

Never leave dogs on balconies or chained in yards, where they may bark or cause a nuisance to others. Chaining dogs seems to increase their frustration and can cause serious aggression problems when they can see passers-by, but not reach them. Many children are bitten after approaching chained dogs that have suffered social neglect and become aggressive.

Communal hallways and entrances are places where proper behaviour will give your dog a good name. Dogs should always be on leads in these areas and should be trained to walk nicely on the lead and sit politely to let other people pass. Your dog should become a local ambassador for her breed and species.

Dogs soon become used to lift travel. Teaching her to sit or stand behind you, near the back or side wall, is usually safest if the lift is crowded.

socialization

the social scene

Every domestic dog has its ancestry in the wolf. From the diminutive Chihuahua to the huge Great Dane, they share genetic material that governs their instincts and behaviour. Although the domestic dog is now as different from his wild cousins as humans are from apes, all dogs need extensive human contact before 12 weeks of age if they are to cope with our city ways.

The critical early days

Puppies learn how to be friendly with people during a very short period of their development: between five and 12 weeks of age. Of course, puppies do continue to learn after this time, but their whole outlook is likely to be affected by their experiences during this period.

A dog that lacks socialization with people, or other dogs, is effectively a wild animal and will experience many behavioural problems throughout his life as he tries to cope with the pressures of living with humans. Socialization occurs very early on in a puppy's life. In fact, pups that are not handled by several different people before the age of 12 weeks are almost certain to lack communication skills as adults.

Of course, dogs see humans as individuals. Can you imagine what a puppy must think when he first meets someone with a beard, wearing glasses or a hat? What do puppies think of children? Kids inevitably look, smell and sound very different from adults, and dogs need to get used to the way they move and act. Even other dogs must look weird, from a puppy's point of view. Just imagine what it must be like for a Dachshund to meet a Golden Retriever for the first time. He has probably grown up with littermates and a mother that all look the same – and suddenly he is confronted by an animal that smells like a dog, but is a different colour and is huge in comparison.

Start as you mean to go on! Chasing the vacuum may seem like fun now, but not when he's three years old.

A puppy's-eye-view of city life

As soon as your puppy is home, he needs to mix with as many people as possible and see the world around him. Even if he has not completed his vaccinations, you can carry him out and about so that he sees and hears the traffic, children's pushchairs and the general hustle and bustle of urban life. Bear in mind that puppies need to be exposed to many different kinds of environment, particularly those that you may visit in the future. This means that trips to the countryside, sea, river or forest may be on the cards.

Urban living is especially challenging for dogs – there are so many things your new puppy needs to become familiar with, or even blasé about. These start in your own home. He will need to be exposed many times to the sound of the vacuum cleaner, washing machine and telephone before he will ignore them. Equally, your puppy needs to know that different sensations underfoot – such as rubber matting, carpet

Urban home checklist

Try to get your puppy used to the following:
- ✔ Vacuum cleaner
- ✔ Washing machine
- ✔ Hair dryer
- ✔ Telephone ringing
- ✔ Food processor
- ✔ Aerosol sprays
- ✔ Carpet/wooden floors
- ✔ Stairs
- ✔ Lifts
- ✔ Mop or broom being used
- ✔ Television
- ✔ Radio
- ✔ Plastic bags being shaken out
- ✔ Collar and lead going on and off
- ✔ Traffic noise from an open window.

and wood – are all safe to stand on. The rule with all new encounters is that you must ignore anxiety or fearful behaviour as much as possible, and reward a brave, confident approach instead, so be generous with praise, attention and treats to let your puppy know when he is behaving in the right way.

Try to think about your domestic environment, as well as the wider range of the city, from your dog's point of view – it is guaranteed to be an eye-opener.

meeting and greeting

As soon as your puppy comes into your home, it is important to build up a relationship with him. This will give him safety and security, as well as laying a foundation on which to base a lifetime of trust and understanding. However, it is healthy for your puppy to share loyalties with other family members, friends and visitors — he should love everybody!

Impulse control

It used to be thought that dogs regarded our families as 'packs' – with a clear structure and hierarchy – but this view has now been challenged. In the wild, where dogs live in social groups, the system is based far more on teamwork than on dominance, with the individual strengths and weaknesses of group members being acknowledged.

Ideally, we need to live with our dogs in this way, too. Although it is wise to set boundaries at the start of your relationship, you do not need to dominate your puppy physically or psychologically. It is far better to train him to know what is acceptable and what is not, and to teach him impulse control. By learning to control his own impulses, your pup will have an outlet for his natural behaviour only when it is appropriate for you and the environment.

Your puppy needs to meet as many different people as possible in the first 12 weeks of his life. Socialization does not stop there, but it does become more difficult if you have missed this critical stage. He also needs to be content when left in the company of other people while you are not there. This helps to prevent any over-attachment problems later in life and gives him a well-rounded social start. For this reason, leaving him with willing members of your family or friends for a day or two can benefit him hugely.

Make sure your puppy meets new people – it can be fun for you too!

Promoting child-friendliness

Puppies need to meet children – especially if you do not have kids at home. Many dogs seem to love children inherently, while others simply put up with them. If you suspect that your dog is merely tolerating the presence of children, it is critical that you make positive associations with them, repeatedly. Giving children titbits to hand to your dog, as well as playing games with him and walking him in the park, can all help. However, beware of letting your puppy become overwhelmed by the attentions of children, particularly if they have congregated en masse or if your dog is tiny. Always prevent children picking up your puppy unless you are watching them carefully.

Getting to know men

Many dog owners report that their puppy is fine with women and children, but seems scared of men. They often comment that perhaps he has been hurt by a man in the past, although this is rarely likely to be the case. The simple fact is that a pup's early contact with people is much more likely to have been with women than with men. Men are also inherently more scary to a puppy – they are bigger, taller and have deeper voices,

which sound more threatening. For all these reasons it is essential that your dog meets as many men as possible in his early weeks and learns to associate them with pleasant things, such as food, walks and calm affection.

Socialization checklist

Progress your puppy's socialization with people and city life by getting him acquainted with the following:

✔ **Adults: a minimum of ten new people of different ethnic origin**
✔ **Children: a minimum of ten (go to an area where lots of children congregate, such as outside a school)**
✔ **Person wearing a hat**
✔ **Person wearing sunglasses**
✔ **Person wearing a crash helmet**
✔ **Person on crutches**
✔ **Person in uniform**
✔ **Person carrying a clipboard or other large item.**

dog in disguise : other pets

There is no reason why your new puppy cannot be best buddies with a resident cat, rabbit or any other animal that you keep as an urban pet. However, those first few hours and days together are critical — so planning how you will manage the introductions, and keeping them calm and controlled, is a sensible strategy.

Cats

Cats are highly sensitive creatures, which show their displeasure or stress in many different ways, including spraying urine in your home or leaving faeces on your duvet. It is essential that even 'dog-proof' cats are allowed to get to know the new puppy in their own time, and that they have an escape route if they feel they need it. This is especially important in the city, where many cats live an indoor existence without ready access to a garden.

During the first few meetings, make sure your pup is on a lead, so that you can prevent him chasing the cat. Such behaviour is extremely self-rewarding, and it only takes one game of chasing the cat upstairs or behind the television for the puppy to repeat the behaviour forever.

are stimulated to chase by movement. This means that just because your dog is good with your rabbit while she is sitting on your knee or in her cage, he may not be so well behaved when she is able to run free in the house or outdoor pen.

Right from the start, you need to build good associations with other pets, so avoid scolding or punishing your puppy. Keep your pet in a cage or hutch to begin with, or your dog securely behind a baby gate, so that both animals can watch and even sniff each other, but cannot make contact. Praise and reward your dog for ignoring the rabbit or guinea pig, and completely disregard any interest or excitement that he shows. Barking may upset your other pet, so keep your puppy quiet by giving him a chew or Kong toy (see pages 130–131), or a Buster™ Cube or activity ball (different shapes that also dispense food treats). Growling or snarling is a bad sign – in this case, stop the introductions and seek professional help.

Birds

Interestingly, the vast majority of dogs learn to ignore birds kept as pets. However, there are reports of some dog breeds showing particular interest in them. Shiba Inu and other similar breeds are well known for their ability to chase and catch birds in flight outdoors, so you need to take the greatest care when introducing a puppy to the idea of cohabiting with any parrots or budgerigars, especially when free flying.

Reptiles

Keeping reptiles as pets is increasingly popular in cities across the world. Although some owners report social interaction between dogs and reptiles, on the whole they are best kept separate, unless the dog is under strict supervision and has been taught to ignore the other pet completely. Some diseases, such as salmonella, can be also transmitted between reptiles, dogs and people, so scrupulous hygiene is essential.

Ideally, give your puppy a chew or an exciting toy to occupy him, and encourage him to settle on the floor next to you, with the lead held loosely. If your cat will come into the same room, make sure she has some tasty food to eat, high up on a vantage point such as a windowsill or shelf. This will help her feel secure and understand that with the puppy come good things. Repeat these brief (but enjoyable) encounters over a number of days. If she won't come into the same room, keep your pup behind a baby gate to help her feel safe and pair all visual contact with delicious food until she feels more secure. It is worth taking your time, because cats and dogs can become great friends if the first introductions are handled carefully.

Rabbits and guinea pigs

Many city dwellers now keep house rabbits and guinea pigs as pets, and they can be taught to coexist happily with a dog, but supervision and training are essential from the beginning, no matter how confident you feel about their friendship. Dogs are predators and most

out and about in the city

Your pup's first outing into the big wide world is bound to be exciting — but it can also be a bit daunting for him, so it's best to be prepared in advance. Vaccination times vary, so check with your veterinarian when it's safe to take your puppy out — but the general rule is: do it as soon as possible.

First forays

All puppies encounter what is known as a 'fear period' — the timing varies from breed to breed and from dog to dog, but usually occurs from about 12 weeks onwards. In the wild this would keep the pups from harm, because a cautious dog is a safe one. However, in a city environment it is vital that puppies become so accustomed to the sights, sounds and smells of the streets that they are unconcerned by them. This means getting your pup out and about just as soon as you can — even if his first forays are in your arms, rather than walking on his own four paws.

Imagine that you are seeing the world from your dog's perspective. Can you visualize what a cacophony of sensations the city must bring: the noise of vehicles, the forest of human legs, and the smells from drains, rubbish bins, restaurants and traffic. Think about how distracting that must be for a dog with his heightened senses. We expect our dogs to be able to cope with all this, and more — and it is up to us to let them know that these experiences are just a part of daily life and are not to be feared. Bear in mind that what your puppy encounters now will impact on his confidence for the rest of his life, so make sure you get out and about before it's too late!

Just like people, dogs vary in confidence levels and a desire to explore, but all puppies need repeated exposure to city life to learn to cope and enjoy their environment.

communication and affection – when he is being confident. The second he starts to look even slightly concerned, all this attention must switch off and he should be kept safe, but effectively ignored.

Repeated exposure

Bear in mind that puppies may find it difficult to multi-task at first. Being taken into a city must be a little like being put on a new planet. If your puppy sits still and refuses to budge, or doesn't want to walk with you, be patient. Pick him up and carry him if necessary, but keep taking him out – it simply means he needs more exposure to city life, not less.

All puppies need repeated trips to as many different places as possible for their confidence to develop, so that nothing surprises them – no matter how new or unusual. To help your puppy meet his new urban world, it can be useful for the whole family to create a checklist of sights, sounds and experiences for him to encounter. Keep adding to the list of adventures and ticking items off, until your dog really is a city slicker!

It's down to you

It is completely natural for a puppy to be slightly overwhelmed by all the new stimuli he will experience on his first excursions into the city. How *you* react will determine whether or not he quickly overcomes his anxieties or is fearful for ever. Puppies watch, listen and learn all the time and look to us for guidance, but don't understand the words we say. While we may be thinking that a pup needs reassurance, it is quite possible that he believes he is being rewarded for being fearful – or, worse, that his owner is scared, too.

For this reason, it is vital that everyone who accompanies your puppy on his first few encounters with city life understands that they must only pay him attention – in terms of eye contact, vocal

City tour checklist

	SEEN	USED
Car	☐	☐
Train	☐	☐
Bus	☐	☐
Bicycle	☐	
Busy pedestrian area	☐	☐
Public area where your puppy had to be calm (such as a café)	☐	☐
Pedestrian crossing	☐	☐
Scooter	☐	
Person on a skateboard	☐	
Person on roller skates	☐	

canine friendships
matter

No matter what type of dog you have, it is vital that he mixes with as many different dogs as possible before he's much older than 16 weeks. Dogs that lack canine company at an early age often fail to learn essential social and communication skills, which can lead to anxiety or even fights later on — so don't let your pup miss out.

Play skills

Ideally, start socializing your puppy with other dogs in your neighbourhood the minute you can, especially if you own a breed that needs above-average socialization. Your vet will advise you when it is safe to take your pup to public places in the city, such as the park, after completing his vaccinations, but even before then playing with other dogs that are vaccinated is generally safe.

Young puppies need to mix with other dogs and play with them, if they are to learn good communication skills for adult life. These skills prevent confrontation and promote social encounters, even between animals that have never previously met. Just like kids at the playground, dogs need to learn how to play nicely, how to share and when to stop and take a break.

Puppy party

Well-run puppy playgroups, or classes, offer such an opportunity in a safe environment and are a great start to your pup's education. They should involve a good balance of play and training, so that owners are not excluded from the fun and your puppy still wants to pay you attention, despite romping with his buddies.

Play between puppies should be balanced. One puppy should not appear to be bullying another, and

A good puppy class should offer both calm training and playtime fun. A maximum of 6–8 puppies is ideal.

a good instructor will intervene if she thinks the play is getting too rough. Your vet should be able to point you in the direction of a good puppy class, but do ask to watch one before attending. Look out for these factors:

✳ Both puppies and people should look relaxed and happy, with the whole family welcome.

✳ Exercises should be broken into small sessions suitable for puppies to learn.

✳ Punitive methods or equipment should not be in use; choke/check chains, tight slip collars and prong collars are not necessary.

✳ Noise should be kept to a minimum – shouting is unnecessary, and lots of barking may indicate that the dogs are stressed.

✳ Instructors should be approachable: do they appear friendly and caring, in the best interests of both owner and pup?

✳ There should not be too many puppies in the class; look at size of the venue, as well as the number of assistants: can the instructor keep an eye on everyone at once?

✳ Methods should suit both the dog and the handler in question; food and toys are excellent motivators – not many dogs work for praise alone.

✳ Play between puppies should be carefully supervised and controlled, and combined with gentle, effective training.

Doggie daycare

Living and working in the city may mean that you are not at home to look after your dog during the day, and doggie daycare may well be the answer. Such daycare centres usually look after dogs during the working day, giving them exercise, training and a chance to be with other dogs. They can be great way for your pup to meet new canine friends – and for owners to socialize, too. Always check with the centre how many dogs they house and how many carers they have on hand. Play between the dogs should always be monitored, and your puppy's social welfare should be paramount.

new horizons: rural life

Although city living takes some getting used to, it is important that your dog can cope in different circumstances, too. Visits to the countryside while your puppy is young are essential, not only for a change of scenery, but so that your dog learns to accept the sights, sounds and smells associated with rural living, just as much as those in his native city.

Visits to the country

Dogs are highly adaptable creatures, but this flexibility is greatly enhanced by giving them varied social experiences while they are young. Becoming familiar with new environments is an essential part of your puppy's education, and although it may seem unlikely to us, the countryside can seem just as daunting as the city, if your puppy is new to it.

Consider which aspects of rural life your pup might need to encounter in future. Do you have friends or relatives who live outside the city? If so, what kinds of experiences might your pup have when visiting them? Some puppies may need to become familiar with a variety of livestock; others may have to learn to cope with the intermittent traffic of a rural area, which is quite different from the constant drone experienced in the city.

The rules of rural visiting are much the same as those that apply in the city: keep your dog on the lead in unfamiliar areas, and make sure that you allow your pup time to assimilate all the new stimuli around him. Humans can rationalize sights such as tractors or sounds such as loud gunshot, but dogs cannot. Refrain from attempting to reassure your pup if he's momentarily startled by something new – instead, praise and reward brave behaviour. Repeated exposure to new areas is always beneficial for your puppy and you should continue it right into adolescence. After all, it's a good excuse for you to take some fresh air and countryside exercise, too.

Is it a dog? Your pup needs to experience the countryside if he's to become familiar with all it has to offer.

basic training

understanding canine motivation

Living and working in the city, most of us know that we do not work for love alone – we need a salary to make the daily grind worthwhile, and the same is true for dogs. Unlike Lassie in the famous film of the same name, dogs need a reason to work for us and to comply with our rules and ideals.

Dog preferences

The key to any training is knowing how to motivate your dog – and understanding her likes and dislikes will impact enormously on your training. Does your dog prefer cheese or chicken, or would she much prefer a good game with a toy to a tasty morsel? Training should be fun, and this means that even if you are using food to motivate your dog, you may need to jazz up the way you use it. If you animate yourself, make noises and look excited, it will add to your puppy's motivation.

Dogs have different preferences, depending on their breed and their own disposition. Generally, Labradors and Retrievers adore food and probably prefer a smelly bit of frankfurter to anything else. However, terriers may choose a good tug game with a rag toy, while Collies and Sheepdogs have a preference for chase games like fetch. Tiny dogs may look as if they will work for love alone – but look again. A lot of dogs don't like being patted on the head, and if you have a tendency to do this to your dog, watch closely her reaction to it. Does she really like it?

Praise is not enough

The fact that dogs don't do what we want for love should not be regarded as a personal insult. It's best to wise up and admit that most dogs won't work for praise alone. Even offering a small reward may not be sufficient in some circumstances. For example, your

dog may work for dry food indoors, but if you are in an environment with lots of distractions – such as walking the city streets or in a training-class situation – you may need to up the stakes. The rewards you are offering for walking nicely next to you, or waiting quietly at the side of the street, must outweigh those rewards that your dog may get from following her own instincts – whether this is rolling in unpleasant substances or pestering strangers for attention.

Training your city dog to do what you want is easy if you remember one rule: what gets rewarded by you gets repeated by her. This means that you need to think about rewards from your dog's point of view. Bear in mind that your pup may love attention so much that laughter, eye contact and even being told off may encourage her to carry out the same behaviour over and over again. For this reason, always consider what your dog is gaining from behaviour that you don't like. For instance, barking at passers-by may give the impression that she's being brave or protective, when in reality she's simply being rewarded by the reaction she causes. Always try to 'think dog'.

Focus and concentration in learning a new task come from motivation to receive a reward, not just a desire to please.

Infinite possibilities

Dogs are intelligent, creative animals that can be taught to perform the most complex and impressive tasks. What you choose to teach your dog will depend on the urban environment, your needs and her enthusiasm. Your pup is more than capable of learning to load and unload the washing machine (one of the easiest tasks they learn to perform for disabled owners), close doors or push the lift call button – but the basics of training for city life must come first.

attention training

The city has so many distractions that it's little wonder your dog would rather be sniffing the air for hot dogs, or looking out for a canine companion in the dog park. Teaching your dog to give you her attention at home is relatively easy, but outside in the urban jungle you will have to fight to become your dog's priority.

Look at me!

Your goal is for your dog to look at you and give you her full attention when you say her name. This might sound easy, but many dogs probably think their name is 'No'! Just watching dogs out and about in the city will make you realize that you have to work hard to compete with the many distractions that urban life throws at you and your dog. Sights, sounds and smells compete for her attention, and the lure of other dogs and playtime in the park can be almost impossible to resist.

Teaching attention at home

It is always best to start attention exercises at home, so that you can perfect them in a relatively stress-free environment. Make sure your home is calm and quiet, so that you can focus on your dog for a few minutes. Training sessions don't need to be long – it's quality, not quantity, that counts.

With your dog in the same room, say her name clearly, in a friendly tone of voice. The instant she looks at you, say 'Good' and give her a tasty reward. Repeat this at least ten times in one session, then have a break. You can then repeat the session several times in one day.

Perfecting the technique

The next stage of your attention training is perhaps the most important. You need your dog to stop whatever she is doing and look at you, no matter where she is or what her brain is engaged in. Practise these steps when your dog is just lying around the home, when she's playing and when she's busy sniffing or looking at something else. You can perfect all this by practising indoors.

Teaching attention in the city

Once you are happy with your dog's standard of responsiveness inside, take the training out into the urban environment. Clearly this is more difficult for your dog, so help her at the outset by keeping her on the lead and waiting for an opportunity when you think success is likely. At the start of training, there is little point in asking her to give you attention when she's gazing at an irresistible canine across the park – you will simply be setting her up for failure. Instead, wait until she's relaxed and then say her name. Help her immediately if she doesn't look at you by producing a wonderful, smelly food treat such as a bit of hot-dog sausage and letting her sniff it; then bring it up to your face so that she has to look at you. As soon as she does, say 'Good' and give her the treat.

It is far better to engineer a positive response with this exercise than to nag your dog for ignoring you. Keep in mind that dogs are bombarded with noises in the city – and particularly with human voices, which they (rightly) learn to ignore. Expecting your dog to pick out the single word in a sentence that applies to her is asking a lot, so give her plenty of help and rewards at the outset.

Practise makes perfect! Ask your dog to give you attention as often as possible in the city.

Up the ante

Ask your dog to sit and look at you before she gets her dinner or a game, or is allowed off-lead in a safe area for exercise and play. Nothing works faster than your city dog understanding that she must give you her attention before she gets the good things in life.

recall training

Training your dog to come when you call can be a lifesaver in the city. For many dogs, the chance to run off-lead is the best thing in their day, acting as a stress-buster for the restrictions of urban life, but you need to know your dog will return on cue. For others, it can mean the difference between life and death, if they manage to escape from the home.

When I'm calling you!

Your dog should come when you call because she believes you are fun to be with and that rewards are on offer. She should never be worried or anxious about returning to you, because in an urban emergency (such as the sudden appearance of a police car with siren blaring) it is essential that she runs towards you for

security, not away from you. For this reason, recall training should never be associated with punishment – no matter how slow your dog is in returning.

Teaching recall in the city

If you are unsure how your dog will respond on the first few occasions outdoors, use a long line or an extending lead. Continue the same routine you have started indoors, but be aware that the more distractions there are from urban life, the better your rewards and praise need to be.

Although most dogs respond well to food treats inside the home where there is little to distract them, outside in city areas where it is safe to allow them to exercise off-lead you may find that other factors side-track them. If this happens, you can scale up your training by getting your dog addicted to playing with a special toy instead. Suitable toys are Frisbees™, raggers and balls on ropes, which enable you to throw the toy with ease, but have a handle that you can hold on to.

Play inside with your dog and her new toy on several occasions, but always put it away after a really good game, so that she's left wanting more. After several games, your dog should be very keen to play with the toy and will be amazed when you suddenly produce it from a pocket while out on a walk. She will then be far keener to come back to you when you call, and will keep an eye on you as she runs around, in the hope of getting a game with it.

Teaching recall at home

Start your recall training indoors where there are few distractions and you can effectively control your dog's movements. Have some really tasty, soft food treats – such as pieces of cooked chicken or cheese – ready in a lidded container, so that you don't have to hold them in your hands.

1 Call your dog in a friendly voice. If she shows no response, clap your hands or make silly noises until she looks at you. Then, using the food as a lure, move backwards one or two paces. If she moves just one step towards you, say 'Good', then give her several treats straight away – putting them on the floor in front of you.

2 Gradually increase the distance your dog has to come to get the treat, making sure that you praise her profusely. Give her delicious rewards and a game with a toy for coming when you call.

3 Now practise calling your dog to you at unusual moments in and around your home, and then in the garden or back yard if you have one. Build up your pup's recall before practising in the park or other open spaces where there are more distractions.

sit in the city

Perhaps the most versatile of all dog-training commands, and the easiest to teach, 'Sit' is a good way of keeping control when your dog would rather bounce; of stopping her walking too far ahead; and of demonstrating her manners at the side of the road. But asking her to sit is only half the battle – getting her to stay in that position is what counts.

Perfecting the sit

It is important to practise the sit in all contexts, both in the relative peace of your home and out and about in the heart of the city. Remember that what you have taught at home needs to be repeated over and over again, in as many different urban situations as possible, for it to be completely reliable. Your dog's responses may seem a

bit slow at first if she's distracted outdoors, but be patient and stick with the programme.

It may seem tempting to push on your dog's rear end if she doesn't respond straight away to your 'Sit' command, but this is counter-productive because it simply teaches her to stay out of reach if she doesn't want to comply.

Sit and stay

Once your dog has learned to sit on cue, you can teach her to stay in that position for longer, simply by waiting before you say 'Good' and give a treat, and by adding in distractions (see below). These need to be fairly gentle to start with – if your dog moves, you know you have done too much too soon; go back to a simpler task and build up the distractions again until you achieve success. Make sure that you keep your dog in position for random amounts of time, building up to about one minute. Praise her all the time she is sitting.

Adding in distractions

✳ With your dog sitting, take two paces away, then move back to her, say 'Good' and give her a treat.
✳ Ask your dog to sit. Put your hands on your head. If she stays, say 'Good' and give her a treat.
✳ Build up to being able to walk all round your dog while she sits and stays. Do this in small stages, and bear in mind that she is most likely to move when you disappear from view as you walk round her tail. Be generous with praise and treats.

Sit!

Some breeds may find it easier to sit on command than others, and this seems to depend on their physical construction. Whippets, Greyhounds and some Lurchers may prefer to stand or lie down rather than sit, but it is not impossible to teach them to sit on cue if you are patient.

1 Show your dog that you have a food treat in your hand. Put it on her nose, right up close. Lift your hand up and back, so that she has to look right up to follow your fingers.

2 The movement of your dog looking upwards like this will cause a physical chain reaction – her rear end has to go down. Say 'Good' and give a reward as soon as this happens. Repeat this a few times. Now say the word 'Sit' just before you move the food lure.

3 Then try it without the lure! With no food in your hand, ask your dog to sit. If she does, say 'Good' immediately, then give her a food treat. If she does not sit when asked, help her with the hand signal, then reward her for her good efforts.

down and roll-over

When your dog is lying down, she is calm and under control. Teaching her to lie down on cue is essential for city living. It ensures she is safe in public, and makes her more approachable for children and those who are not confident around dogs. It signals your commitment to training, for the good of your dog and people you meet.

Perfecting the down

In the initial stages of training, dogs often try other behaviour before lying down. Your dog might stand up again – in which case your hand was probably too far away from her. She might raise one paw to try and get the food, or might lower her front end to the floor, leaving her rear end in the air. All you need to do is wait: eventually her back end will flop down to the floor too, and you can reward your dog.

Down and stay

To train your dog to stay in the down position, simply delay the number of seconds before you say 'Good' and give her the food treat. Work up from five seconds to start with, to a whole minute or even two. Test the stability of her 'Down stay' by standing up or sitting down yourself. Clap your hands, kneel on the floor and turn round. Does she stay? If so, she's ready to practise outside in the distracting world of the city.

Roll-over!

Teaching your dog a trick may seem like frivolity to us, but to your pet it's just one more skill that she learns, and a chance to build her relationship with you. Roll-over is a great one to start with because it's relatively simple, fun and looks great when performed with finesse.

Start by asking your dog to lie down. Once she is down, watch which way her hips are angled. Using a food treat close to the side of her mouth, lure the dog's head over her own shoulder, so that she is looking backwards. Follow through with the food treat, while the dog flops onto her back and then rolls right over. Remember to say 'Good' and give her a tasty treat for being so clever.

Add the words 'Roll-over' only when she is reliably and voluntarily offering the behaviour, and perfect the trick by practising until your dog can dive into a roll-over from a standing position, then stand back up again. This looks really impressive – your city friends will be amazed.

Down!

Training your dog to lie down on command will take a little practice and patience. Once again, there is no need for force or physical pressure to get your dog to comply – indeed, it is very important that you have control of her mind, and not just her body. Ensure you have plenty of tasty food treats to hand.

1 With your dog sitting, hold a food lure close to her nose. Lower your hand slowly down to the floor, directly between her front paws. Hang on to the treat by turning your palm down, with the food hidden inside your hand. In this way your dog will want to burrow her nose underneath and will turn her head sideways to nibble at it.

2 Be patient and your dog will soon lie down. The instant she does, say 'Good', then drop the treat on the floor and let her eat it (this prevents the dog following your hand back up again like a yo-yo).

3 Repeat this several times. Alternate between having the food in your hand and not having it there, but always give a treat when she lies down. Once you can guarantee that your dog will lie down by following your hand to the floor, you can add in the word 'Down' just *before* you move the lure.

look, but don't touch!

Teaching your dog not to touch things on cue is an essential requirement of our modern urban lifestyle. Unfortunately, our city streets are often covered in unmentionable items that you definitely don't want your dog to touch, let alone swallow. A reliable 'Leave' command is an essential part of surviving street culture.

Perfecting the leave

Extend the exercise by practising with food in your hand, on surfaces and on the floor. Over a number of repetitions, dogs of all ages learn very rapidly that the word 'Leave' means that they must not touch. This training exercise needs to be started by adults.

Children can take over the training only once the dog understands that trying to snatch the food from you is ineffective. For dogs that are determined to use their teeth or claws to get at the food in your hand, a glove offers good protection at the outset.

Training to leave things outside

In order to make this exercise really reliable out in the city, practise walking around indoors, dropping items such as pieces of paper or dry food treats. Tell your dog to 'Leave', then get eye contact to ensure that she's thinking about you, and not the item. As soon as she does this, say 'Good' and give a far better treat than the one that she's resisted. Implement your new training on the city streets only when you feel confident that it has become reliable at home.

Think about all the many things you don't want your dog to touch in the urban environment. Rubbish is apparent everywhere, and food lies on every street corner. However, you can also teach your dog to ignore squirrels, cats, other dogs and even children by using the 'Leave' command.

Warning!

Most dogs learn this exercise incredibly fast and it can be made very reliable over a number of repetitions. However, dogs are designed to be scavengers, which means that if you leave food out unsupervised at home, they will eat it.

Leave!

As with all new exercises, it is best to teach your dog to leave items on command by starting at home, where there are few distractions. Once she has mastered the exercise at home you can venture out on to the street.

1 Hold a treat in your hand and close your fingers tightly around it. Present your hand to your dog and wait while she sniffs, licks and nibbles, trying to get at the food. Do not say anything, but watch carefully. As soon as your dog takes her nose away from your hand – even for a split second – say 'Good' and then release the treat. Repeat this several times. Most dogs learn to take their mouth away from your hand in about four tries.

2 Now you can wait until your dog has taken her nose away from your hand for the count of three, then say 'Good' and give her a treat. Lots of dogs turn their face away as if to resist temptation. Say 'Good' and treat!

3 Build up to about ten seconds the amount of time that your dog will wait with her nose well away from your hand. At this point you can add in the command 'Leave'. Say this in a calm, quiet voice, not a threatening one, before your dog sees the food. Once she has got the hang of this, repeat the exercise, but this time say 'Leave', then present the food on your *open* hand. If your dog tries to take it, simply close your fingers around the food – do not jerk your hand away.

perfecting social visits

Imagine going to your friends for coffee, or meeting up at a café for a social gathering. Although everyone is pleased to see your dog and is happy to greet her, very quickly the conversation turns to other topics and your dog is best seen and not heard. Dogs need to learn that sometimes their owners require them to lie quietly without demanding attention.

Settle down!

Teaching your dog to settle down on cue is easy. All you need is patience and consistency. The best way to teach this command is at home, when everything else is relatively quiet.

Attach your dog's lead, and take her somewhere that you would like to sit – the lounge area is ideal. Sit down in a chair and make yourself comfortable.

Say 'Settle down' to your dog in a quiet voice, then place her lead under your foot, so that she can stand, sit and lie down in comfort, but her options are otherwise limited.

Most dogs will try to get your attention by whining, pulling on the lead or pawing at you. This is where you need to possess strong resolve. Do not look at your dog, talk to her or touch her. After a few minutes and several efforts to get your attention, most dogs simply give up and lie down with a huge sigh of resignation. This is exactly what you are looking for. Praise her gently, then stay like this for a few minutes before ending the session with the word 'Finish' and taking off the lead.

Perfecting the technique

You need to practise this technique every night for about a week for it to become reliable, but it's worth it. There are literally hundreds of times that you will be thankful you taught 'Settle down' on command: in the vet's waiting room, at a café, in other people's homes, and just when you've had a hard day in the city and want to relax in front of the television. This is one command that should be compulsory for city dogs everywhere.

'Settle down' is not a formal 'stay' position – indeed some owners prefer to use the cue 'Chill' or 'Relax'.

on the lead

heel with me

Teaching your dog to walk on a loose lead on city streets is imperative. There's nothing more embarrassing or more hazardous than a dog pulling your arm out of its socket while you try to maintain control. Dogs that pull on-lead tend to be taken out for walks less frequently, making them more frustrated and unruly — creating a vicious circle for you both.

Get it right

The main reason why so many dogs pull on the lead is that they get rewarded for it. Dogs quickly work out that by pulling, they get to the park more quickly and can lead their owners wherever they want to go, rather than the other way round.

For this reason, you need to start your dog's lead-training in a calm, quiet place, not when you are trying to run round the city streets doing chores or when you are under pressure from time or the weather. Many people find this exercise difficult because they simply don't put in enough practice. If your dog never goes on-lead, you can't expect him to know how to behave properly.

Dogs need information about when they are in the right place while walking nicely on the lead, and this is where a voice marker really comes into its own. Rather than telling the dog off for pulling, take away all his fun by simply standing still. When the dog is in the right place, let him know by saying 'Good' – thus marking the right behaviour – and giving a treat, then moving forward.

Perfecting the heel

Walking nicely on the lead is probably the most difficult exercise for many dogs to master, and although your dog may become proficient at this very rapidly at home, outside is a different matter. Puppies often just want to sit in the street and gaze at all the marvels the city has to offer, while older dogs may try to plough their way through the crowded pavements to get to the dog park.

Power steering in the city

If your dog pulls like a train, or if you are short on time and high on stress, take a sensible option and use a head collar to walk your dog. This works like a halter on a horse and, when properly fitted, is comfortable for you and your dog. Never use choke chains, choke collars or prong or spike collars.

Walking your dog on a loose lead

Put your dog on a flat, buckle collar and an ordinary lead in your lounge, hallway or garden. Stand still to begin with, and hold the lead close to your body to prevent your hand being pulled towards the dog. Do not take a single step if there is any tension in the lead and do not let your hand fly out away from your body. Focus on encouraging your dog to follow you – there should be no reliance on the lead at all; keep him guessing as to where you are going and when he will be rewarded, and he will be at heel without needing any force.

1 Hold a food treat in your hand closest to your dog. Let him know it's there. As soon as he puts slack in the lead and looks at you, say 'Good' and treat him.

2 Walk just one or two steps in any direction you choose. Watch your dog's position carefully. If there is any tension in the lead, stand still or suddenly change direction. Do not take one single step in the direction your dog wants to go if the lead is tight.

3 Every time there is slack in the lead, say 'Good' and treat him. Repeat this several times, then stop and have a game. Be generous with the treats to begin with, then gradually reward only the best responses.

an on-lead view
of the city

One of the greatest untold secrets of dog training is that dogs like pulling on the lead! They do so because they gain rewards from it, while we are left trailing behind them trying to hang on to our control and dignity. From your dog's point of view, pulling on-lead means that _he_ chooses where to go, which direction to head in and how fast.

Urban distractions

Of course, given free rein most sensible city dogs would wind up somewhere in the vicinity of free food, fun and games or the chance to run off-lead. This means that if your dog pulls you in the direction of the nearest street vendor and finds lots of delicious leftovers to scavenge, or drags you to the dog park and then gets to go off-lead with his buddies, he's guaranteed to do it again.

Keeping your dog's view of the city firmly in mind while training on-lead walking is essential while you are out and about in any urban environment, but especially with a puppy. Learning to be aware of potential hazards is vital for your dog's safety, but looking out for distractions that can wreak havoc with your training is also important.

City hazards

As upright human beings, we rarely stop to consider what it must be like to walk so close to the ground. This means that we tend to avoid obstacles that may be in our path, such as street signs, but which are not obvious to our dogs; meanwhile we happily walk them straight into hazards that they can see, but which we cannot – such as the open grilles on drain covers. This must be especially disconcerting for small dogs.

Being on-lead means that our dogs are effectively at our mercy. Pulling or yanking them suddenly in an unexpected direction must be at least uncomfortable, and at worst potentially damaging to their neck and spine. Many dogs that pull on the lead do so not because they are pulling *towards* something, but because they are trying to get away from us. This is especially the case where a dog's collar or lead is causing discomfort, and is another reason to avoid the use of choke chains or prong or spike collars.

A world of scent

Dogs live in a world of scent that we can hardly imagine. Olfactory messages left by other dogs on street corners and against fire hydrants or lamp posts are the canine equivalent of Post-it notes – telling the reader the gender, sexual status, health and possibly even the age of the sender. For this reason, dogs are inevitably attracted to sniffing where other dogs have been. Indeed, on occasions when the scent message is really rich, the dog may even want to 'taste' it with the special Jacobson's organ in the roof of his mouth (see page 32). This behaviour is characterized by the dog sniffing deeply, then drooling and chattering his teeth at the same time as he draws the chemical odour over the organ to gain more information. This is usually seen in entire males that are interested in finding receptive bitches.

Dogs are so entranced by scent signals that you should not be surprised when your pup wants to drag you towards them. However, such bad-mannered behaviour is not inevitable. Just as you can refrain from suddenly dragging your dog towards the corner shop or vending machine, so your dog can learn to control his impulses to stop and sniff at every tree and post. Dogs do not need to scent mark every few paces – indeed this can increase tension between dogs in the neighbourhood. Train him to have some self-control by making it a rule that you only stop twice on a walk – and only when *you* say that he can. You will be glad you made this rule when you are walking in the rain.

Embarrassing, uncomfortable and even dangerous – but not inevitable! Dogs of all shapes and sizes can be taught to walk politely on the lead.

roadside drill

Dogs are not born with 'traffic sense', and even after a lifetime in the city they are still just as prone to being involved in a road accident as a new puppy. As their carers, we need to make sure that our dogs are safe near the road at all times, by following a roadside drill the whole family can use.

Handling traffic

Road safety should be at the top of owners' training priorities. Dogs need to be calm and confident when they are near traffic and by the road. Bear in mind that, to your dog, different types and levels of traffic will cause different responses and reactions. It may be that

he can cope easily with the sight and sound of cars going by, but that lorries and buses – particularly when they use their air brakes – are another matter.

Many dogs handle traffic easily and quickly, especially if they have been exposed to it in a controlled way from a young age. However, some experience great anxiety and fear, and may hide, try to run or tremble; alternatively, they may simply display body language that shows they are unhappy, by putting their ears back and their tail between their legs. A few dogs – herding types in particular – try to cope with the onslaught of traffic by lunging at passing cars or trying to chase them.

Coping with nervous dogs

If your dog shows mild anxiety at the sight, sound and smell of traffic, you can take action by simply exposing him to the stimuli in a safe way. Sit by a relatively quiet road and let your dog realize gradually that he is not going to be harmed. It may be tempting to cuddle or reassure him during these sessions, but that may serve to reward his fear; so praise and pet him only when he is being brave and ignoring the traffic completely.

If your dog shows extreme fear or is trying to chase the traffic, fit a head collar or body harness for safety reasons, and seek advice from a professional trainer or behaviour specialist. It can take many weeks and months to calm such dogs in the presence of traffic, and the risks to road users, to you and to your dog are considerable if the problem is not handled carefully.

Cross with care

All puppies and older dogs should be taught basic roadside manners, to ensure that you can cross the road safely without being dragged – or dragging! Dogs should wait, preferably in a sit position, until they are told they can cross, when they should walk smartly to heel without pulling or hesitation. It takes some practise, but eventually your dog should start to offer automatic sits when you approach the kerb.

1 Make sure your dog is relaxed and that you are at a good point to cross the road, with clear visibility in both directions. Move well away from parked cars, which can obscure your view and that of oncoming motorists, who won't see your dog if he's tucked behind a parked vehicle.

2 Using a food treat to keep your dog's attention, lead him to the kerb and ask him to sit. Feed him intermittently if there is a lot of traffic and you need to wait. Keep him focused on you until you are ready to cross.

3 When it is safe to walk across the road, give him a command such as 'Cross now' and move off smartly so that he comes with you. Keep a watch for traffic all the time. Give your dog verbal praise for crossing calmly, and a treat if he walks on a loose lead.

dealing with distractions

The city is full of distractions for your dog, which can be both challenging and enjoyable. It is lovely when people want to stop and admire him, but if you are in the middle of a training exercise it can also be problematic. The answer is to train your dog in situations that will prepare him for urban interventions in all its many forms.

People wanting to stroke your dog

In theory, people who want to stroke your dog should ask first, then let him sniff their hand before petting your dog on the chest. In practice, people will put their hand straight on top of his head, without warning. In order to prepare your dog for the fast pace of urban life, it is a good idea to practise putting your hand on his head at home, then giving him a food treat. If you make this into a game, he will start to think that having human hands on his head is a reward to be enjoyed, not something to be avoided.

People offering food to your dog

Nurturing is a way that humans demonstrate affection, so if someone offers your dog food when you are out and about, try not to be cross with them. Of course, it is best if your dog does not eat food he finds on the street or may be given by people in cafés or in the park. The ideal response is usually to tell the other person politely that your dog is on a restricted diet and cannot be given titbits. You can also work on teaching your dog to refuse food unless it is deliberately given by you, using the 'Leave' exercise (see pages 80–81).

Other dogs approaching

Despite our best attempts at gentle and positive socialization, occasionally your training may be tested by a strange dog rushing up to your pet. If the other dog appears friendly, it is often best to allow your dog to have a loose lead and to say hello in as natural a way as possible. However, if the other dog appears to be threatening, or has no owner present, the best that you can do is keep your own dog's attention focused on you, by asking for a sit and then keeping eye contact with him. This tends to defuse the situation. If you have a small dog, beware of picking him up if another dog approaches – this can encourage the other dog to jump up at you, and prevents the two dogs greeting in a natural fashion.

Children running and screaming

City life means being in close proximity to other people and lots of children: often playing in the school playground or cycling in the street or park. This can present a major dilemma for dogs new to urban living, which may view the noises and movements that children make as either frightening or exciting. Getting, and maintaining, your dog's focus on you – together with frequent, calm exposure to kids who are running around – is the answer here. You need to make sure that your dog views these sights and sounds as routine and simply a part of his daily life.

Sudden noises: sirens and alarms

Unexpected noises, police sirens and car alarms are all part of city life. While humans get so used to these interruptions that we barely hear them, your dog's acute sense of hearing will mean that he finds them hard to ignore. Remember that your dog will take his lead from you. If you react, so will he. If you are calm and ignore the noise, he will too.

Working with distractions is just a part of living in the city – remaining calm and relaxed in all situations will help your dog feel the same.

using an extending lead

There are plenty of urban areas where your dog may be able to enjoy some freedom, but still needs to be kept under control and within a safe circumference from you. In these situations, the use of an extending lead can be highly beneficial, but it does come with some strict health-and-safety rules.

Using an extending lead can give your dog freedom, without the risks that are associated with being off-lead in a city area highly populated with people, traffic and other dogs. However, using such a lead requires both proficiency and awareness, and there are certain dos and don'ts to be aware of.

Extending leads can be useful, but do ensure you remain aware of your surroundings at all times.

Dos

✱ Do allow your dog to meet and greet other dogs where appropriate, without putting strain on the lead, as this can alter his behaviour towards other dogs and make him appear rather threatening in his approach.

✱ Do be aware of environmental hazards in the cityscape – getting the lead wrapped round parking meters, trees or other people and dogs could be dangerous for both of you.

✱ Do warn your dog when he is about to get to the end of the line. You can do this by calling 'Stop' – and then half applying the brake. This makes a sound that your dog will learn means slow down, and it will save him from having the lead tug on his neck when the line is fully extended.

Don'ts

✱ Don't grab at the line itself no matter what's happening. This can result in very nasty cuts to your hands or fingers, because under pressure the line can act like wire.

✱ Don't allow the line of the lead to cross the paths of cyclists, joggers or people on rollerblades or skateboards; it can act like a garrotte.

✱ Don't be tempted, if you have a small dog, to lift him off the ground using the lead and collar – always give support under the dog's rear end when picking him up.

living with
your dog

at large in the city

City living often means that we have divided loyalties. We want to spend time with our dogs, but also need to keep contact with friends and enjoy the social life the city has to offer. To achieve the best of both worlds, it's wise to train your dog so that she can accompany you as much as possible when you are out and about.

Shopping opportunities

Just because you love your dog does not mean you have to give up your love of shopping! Some malls and shops do allow dogs in, as long as they are well behaved and under strict control. Remember that not everyone loves dogs, and shop staff may be particularly concerned about damage to stock or shop fittings. Even hairs on an outfit can render it unsaleable, so make sure you keep your dog's nose to herself!

Many malls and shopping centres are large open spaces, often with remarkable acoustics and slippery floors. From a dog's point of view, these factors must be very odd indeed. Your dog will need to become accustomed to this unique environment in the same way that she does to other facets of the city – she will need repeated visits if she is to accept it as a part of her normal routine. What greater excuse could there be for shopaholics!

Café society

What could be a better way of socializing your puppy or dog than sitting in a relaxing pavement café or drinking a coffee on a bench in the city centre? In theory, your dog should settle quietly at your feet, untroubled

Handling stairs

Although it seems strange to us, dogs often have trouble coping with stairs on the first few occasions they encounter them. If your puppy hasn't climbed stairs before, take it slowly and use lots of encouragement. Most dogs manage to go upstairs relatively easily, but coming down seems much more frightening. Never drag your dog downstairs. Instead, put a titbit where she can see it on a lower step and give her time and praise when she makes an attempt.

Once she works out how to come downstairs safely, the opposite problem often occurs and you may find yourself being dragged down them head-first. For safety, use a head collar if you have a large or strong dog, in combination with training. Keep your dog behind you as you come down and tell her to wait after every step, then give a reward for doing so.

If you train her to behave appropriately, your dog will make an excellent companion at a café. It is as well to check what is under the table if you want to settle her there.

by passers-by and happy to greet calmly those who want to come and say hello. Unfortunately, the reality may be a little different if you haven't done your homework. For this reason, practise sitting in a chair at home and asking your dog to settle down (see page 82). Once out and about, go into the same routine, but make sure you keep hold of your dog's lead when you are outside the home. It is distinctly unwise to rely on the strength of a chair or table leg, and all too easy to forget that you have the lead under your foot if you get caught up in conversation.

A dog's-eye-view of street culture from a café is very different from yours. Check that the floor under your table isn't strewn with litter, broken glass or discarded bits of food. If you love your coffee and regular chats with your friends, taking a small mat with you for your dog to sit on will ensure her safety and will also give her a clear signal about what she is expected to do. Shoulder carriers for small dogs are now in vogue. These may keep your pet safe, but do restrict natural socialization.

travel log: car

Car travel is an inevitable part of city and town life. Even if you don't own a car, there are times when your dog will need to get in and out of one and sit politely in the back without barking, spinning round or creating a dangerous distraction. For this reason, start car travel early on with your puppy and teach her some in-car etiquette.

Your dog needs to learn that she travels in the back of the car, in a crate or on the back seat wearing a seatbelt harness. Do not allow her to ride on the passenger seat or unrestrained behind you. In the event of an accident this can have appalling consequences for your dog and for your own safety.

Getting into the car

Teaching your adolescent and adult dog to get into the car should be simple, but many owners still find themselves lifting their 30 kg (66 lb) dog in and out when she's 18 months old. Of course, you should lift small dogs and puppies into the car and restrain them in a suitable way. However, if you own an adolescent of a large breed, you need to teach her to put her front feet up on the edge of the opening, then wait while you lift her rear end in. Once she is adult, you can place some treats in the back of the car and encourage her to get 'Up', then wait while she works it out.

Car etiquette

Never let your dog stick her head out of the window while you are driving. Although this may look cute, it can result in injuries from debris that is blown into the dog's eyes. Dogs that bark at passers-by, cyclists or other vehicles are being allowed to practise defensive behaviour, and this needs to be prevented if it is not to infect other areas of their lives or cause distraction and danger to other road users.

Getting out of the car

Your dog should be completely under your control when getting out of the car – every time. There are no excuses for your dog to jump out unless you have asked her to: this is a vital safety rule. Imagine that your car breaks down, or that you have a puncture in a front tyre on the motorway. You will need to get your dog out of the back of the car in order to wait for the breakdown recovery vehicle, or to reach the spare tyre. Getting your dog out of the car under these precarious conditions will make you grateful that you taught her to be under perfect control, and will mean that a crisis does not quickly become a disaster.

1 With your dog in the vehicle and on-lead for safety, open the hatch or the door, just a fraction. Tell your dog in a firm voice to 'Wait'. If her nose comes towards the opening, immediately close the door again. Be careful not to trap your dog's nose in the door – it just needs to close in front of her. Repeat this procedure until your dog understands that moving forward results in the door closing, while moving backwards means that you open the door. Most dogs work out within six repetitions how to control their own behaviour.

2 Open the door fully. Your dog should stay put. Reach in and hold her lead. If she moves, shut the door again. However, if she waits, you can give the command 'Out' and encourage her out with the lead. Bright dogs work this system out very quickly, but you must reinforce it by being consistent each and every time you take your dog in the car. Never let your pet jump out of the car until you have her lead in your hand and have told her that she may exit.

travel log: other transport

Although you may not initially anticipate it, your dog may need to travel on many different forms of transport during her urban life. Trains, trams, buses, planes and even boats may feature if you are dedicated to taking your dog with you wherever possible. Accustoming her to coping with such experiences takes time and patience, but is well worth it in the end.

Trains and trams

Travelling by train, or even tram, with your dog can be fun and relaxing. With no pressure to concentrate on the road, you can simply enjoy your dog's company and the admiring glances you will get from people when they see how well behaved she is! Teaching your dog to settle down on command is vital for this kind of travel (see page 82). Your dog should not attempt to get on the seats, climb on other passengers or lunge at them as they walk past – no matter how friendly her intentions.

You can carry small dogs in a pet carrier if this is more convenient for you. Many are soft and lightweight, and simply zip together when needed. They provide security and home-from-home comforts for your dog in strange surroundings. Accustoming your dog to the carrier before you use it is essential. Apply the same process as familiarizing your dog with a crate (see pages 42–43), take your time and make sure your pet is really comfortable inside the carrier before you lift it.

Exiting trains and trams can be tricky if your dog has not been trained to wait until you give her the command. You can do this by teaching 'Wait' by the door, and can practise it in your own home for use in

Train travel can be hectic and stressful for humans, so make sure you prepare your dog for the sights and sounds early on if she's to become familar with it.

various situations. As you prepare to disembark from the train, get your dog into a sit next to you (see pages 76–77). Once you are ready to depart, give her the command 'Out' and lead her off the train. Once on the platform, ask her to sit again if you need to organize your luggage or get your bearings. Your dog should remain calm and steady until you are ready to move off.

Planes and overseas travel

More and more dogs are now going on holiday with their owners, to increasingly far-flung lands. Pet passports have been introduced in many countries to enable dogs to cross borders without the need for quarantine. In order to comply with the many regulations this entails, you must check with your veterinary surgeon at least six months before you intend to travel. Airlines do accept dogs, but they nearly always need to travel in a crate in the hold.

Pet taxis

Many cities now offer pet taxi services, to transport your dog to and from the groomer, doggie daycare (see pages 66–67) or the vet. This can be a wonderful boon for busy owners, but do make sure that you have seen just how your dog will be transported and who will be handling her, before saying goodbye.

Travel sickness

Many puppies are travel-sick when they first ride in a car. In most cases, this is simply motion sickness, but it may be compounded by anxiety. Making frequent, short trips when your pup has an empty stomach is the best cure, because – just like children – dogs do grow out of this habit once they become familiar with the effect of the car's motion.

Canine carriers

Recent city fashions have dictated that every owner of a Gucci handbag should also have a Chihuahua or a tiny Yorkshire Terrier to go in it. While carrying your dog about town in a bag may keep her from being trodden on or harried on crowded streets, it does prevent her from behaving like a dog. Dogs need to sniff, walk, run, socialize with other dogs and greet people – and all these behaviours are limited by being carried. If you use a canine carrier, do make sure your pet gets to express natural behaviours during the rest of her day – it's essential.

canine workout:
on the run

Ensuring that you give your dog enough exercise is a priority, but in the city it can certainly be a challenge. Once round the block may be enough for you at the end of a hard day, but it's certainly not sufficient for most dogs. Finding ways that you can enjoy exercise together is the key to making sure you both get the maximum benefit.

How much is enough?

Calculating just how much exercise your dog needs is not an exact science. The amount you give will depend on your dog's age, breed, overall fitness and what else in her day provides mental and physical stimulation.

The duration and type of exercise will also be influenced by the climate – in hot areas your dog's tolerance of exercise will be much reduced, as overheating can be a potentially dangerous health risk.

As a general rule, fit adult dogs can take as much exercise as you can give them, but your dog will need a minimum of two 30–45-minute walks a day – preferably with one that includes off-lead running. The exceptions to this are the giant breeds, which benefit from shorter, more frequent walks rather than long ones. Obviously, tiny dogs will need less exercise – their length of leg alone means that they have to walk less far, but don't be fooled by the size of some of the smaller breeds, such as Miniature Schnauzers or Jack Russells – they love exercise and need it just as much as the bigger breeds.

Puppies primarily benefit from going out for socialization. This means that little and often is best in terms of walks. Of course it's good to let them expend some energy too, but they should not be over-exercised, particularly by jogging on hard ground, which can damage unformed joints. A lack of exercise in pups can cause problems, however, as their joints and bones need some resistance in order to develop properly.

Doggie jogging

Running with your dog requires some preparation. The first rule is that your dog must not pull on the lead. For many runners, it is better to be able to attach the lead to their belt rather than hold it, and this means that for safety reasons your dog must know how to walk on-lead (see pages 84–85). Special belt leads are available that leave your hands free while running and these can be useful for urban exercise. However, your dog simply needs to know that pulling in any direction will fail, while running next to you will gain rewards. As with any exercise programme, your dog needs to build up her fitness and stamina in running. Start with as little as one minute of jogging, then walk for two minutes. Alternate this pattern to build your dog's fitness and understanding of the process. Build up gradually so that you can run further at one stretch, but watch your dog closely for signs of tiring and overheating. It's vital that she enjoys it, too.

1 Keep a careful eye on your dog as you start to run. Is she pacing it, or trying to gallop? It is important that your dog gets into a rhythmic stride next to you as you jog, in order to be comfortable.

2 Bear in mind that once she is running, your dog will not be able to anticipate when you are going to stop. So give her a verbal warning, and then slow down before you turn round, get to a junction or stop for an obstruction.

3 Even if you run on the spot while you stop at a junction or cross a road in the city, your dog should still follow kerbside procedure. She should sit and wait until you give her the command that she can cross (see pages 88–89), and this roadside drill should be totally under your control.

canine workout:
on land and water

Until your city develops a gym where you and your dog can exercise together, you need to find ways of keeping fit that are both challenging and fun. Your dog's view of what is exciting may not be the same as yours, and some breeds are more couch potato than gym bunny. If your dog seems less than keen, find ways of harnessing her natural instincts.

Cycling

Cycling with your dog may seem an idyllic way of enjoying fresh air while exercising your pet. For some dogs, it can indeed be a way to bring them to the peak of fitness, but for the vast majority it is pretty hard work. Dogs are designed to travel long distances by pacing – this is faster than a walk, but slower than a run. Pacing conserves energy and is comfortable for your dog, but this can be difficult to achieve if you are on a bike next to her.

You need to perfect pacing your dog next to you on a bike before you ever consider cycling with her in city areas where the hazards of traffic, pedestrians, other cyclists and dogs can be all too close. Special shock-absorbing springs are available to enable you to attach your dog's lead to a bike – these make any sideways movement from the dog less likely to cause you to wobble; but do take great care to avoid accidents where either you or your dog could end up getting hurt. Dogs need to be able to maintain a slack lead while next to you on the bike. Pulling is not only dangerous for you – it can mean your dog strains muscles and joints.

Exercising your dog with a bike needs careful control. It's important that your dog is physically fit and over one year of age.

Dog-related clubs and activities

Busy cities often feel like impersonal places, ironically with few chances to meet other people with common interests. All that changes when you get a dog, for other dog owners are usually happy to share conversations about their favourite topic. As an extension of this, those who have discovered the joys of dog sports often join a canine club or association that gives them the chance to interact with other like-minded people and enjoy the company of other dogs.

There is a huge variety of different clubs, societies and associations with which to become involved. Some may be competitive, in that they organize dog shows, events or contests; others are simply for fun. The most popular doggie activities normally include agility – where dogs learn how to negotiate various obstacles, such as the 'dog walk' or tunnel; flyball, which is a fast and frantic combination of hurdles and retrieving; and even doggie dancing, where your dog learns to perform tricks in time to a piece of music.

Rollerblading

Rollerblading with your dog carries the same kind of health warnings – being pulled along at top speed by your Ridgeback may seem like a good idea, until she sees a squirrel! Ultimate control is required.

Treadmills

Just occasionally dogs are subjected to being tied to treadmills in the name of exercise. These are very unpleasant for your dog and can lead to muscle strain, overheating and exhaustion. Treadmills may be good for humans in the gym, but they are not in your dog's best interests.

Swimming

Swimming is great exercise and many dogs love it. It is low-impact exercise and offers certain breeds or types of dog an outlet for their natural water-retrieving instincts; it is also the perfect way to cool down on hot days. Lakes and pools may be available in some city parks, or you may be lucky enough to have a purpose-built doggie swimming pool in your area. Some of these allow owners to swim alongside their dogs – an experience akin to swimming with dolphins. Dogs are not usually permitted in city fountains or water features, so do exercise discretion in these areas.

taking your dog to work

Taking your dog to the office would once have been an outrageous suggestion, but with the pressures of modern city living, enlightened companies are recognizing that allowing a well-behaved pet to come to work can have an uplifting effect on staff morale. But in order to be accepted into the firm, your dog must adhere to a strict code of conduct.

Working hound

Clearly dogs can only be accepted at work on a regular basis where the nature of the business permits. However, there are plenty of jobs where dogs are not only tolerated, but actually add to the company spirit. There are some obvious parameters concerning your dog's welfare and the needs of co-workers or customers. In order to become a happy working hound, your dog will need:

✱ A place to be taken out for toilet breaks and exercise at lunch time: this may sound obvious, but all dogs need comfort breaks during the day, and the worst possible misdemeanour an office dog can make is to have an accident in a public area. This need also requires that you, as the owner, are committed to taking your dog out, no matter how busy you are in the office. Dogs are creatures of routine, and if you teach your pet that her toilet break is at a certain time, she will need you to offer it consistently.

✱ A calm and secure place to sleep or rest while you are hard at work: when properly trained, dogs learn simply to settle down and snooze while their owners are working away. While some dogs will happily tuck themselves under a desk, others need

The office dog – a valued member of the team or a noisy nuisance?

to be contained or restricted in some way, if they are not to get into mischief while you are on the phone or otherwise distracted. Using a crate (see pages 42–43) may offer this security – and certainly prevents the embarrassment of your dog eating your colleague's sandwiches.

✳ The ability to amuse herself for long periods without requiring attention: your dog needs to be able to chew or play with a toy quietly by herself while you are busy. This is easily taught (see pages 130–131), but does require some practice. Bringing toys and chews already prepared from home will assist greatly with this (see pages 130–131).

✳ Access to water at all times: this is an obvious need for your dog, but a potentially problematic one in a busy office. Keep water bowls out of the way of foot traffic, and ensure that they are well clear of cables and electrics.

✳ A sociable and friendly temperament: even if you are the boss, it is terribly unfair to inflict a difficult, noisy or unpredictable dog on your co-workers or customers. Not everyone likes dogs, and you should keep this in mind when you explore whether it is a good idea to take your dog to work with you. There is never an excuse for any disruptive or aggressive behaviour in the workplace – and this goes for dogs as well as humans!

✳ The ability to remain quiet, no matter what is happening around her: talking on the phone, being able to focus and concentrate, and welcoming guests into the work environment all require that your dog stays calm and quiet. Of course, most dogs want to bark when someone new enters their territory, so it takes a good deal of work and effort if this is not to become a habit. Practising this behaviour at home will help – teaching your dog to go and lie down when someone arrives, rather than jumping up at them or barking, is an essential first step (see page 109).

Take-to-work checklist

✔ A lead for restraint where necessary
✔ Chews and toys to keep your dog occupied
✔ A towel – essential for wiping paws and jowls
✔ A discreet clean-up kit, including bags, paper towels, cleaning products and air freshener
✔ Canine first-aid kit in case of emergency
✔ A portion of your dog's daily feed – in case you need to stay late at the office
✔ Treats in a sealed tin, for rewarding perfect office manners
✔ A non-spill water bowl.

polite dog-park behaviour

In general, an off-lead recreation area or dog park is an outdoor space where dog owners can let their pets run free. It may be fenced or unfenced, ranging in size from 0.4 hectares (1 acre) to a vast area. It may have water, restrooms, shelters, trees – or no facilities at all. Above all, it has dogs, who need to be on their best behaviour.

Entering and leaving the dog park

Most dog parks, especially in cities, have double-gated entries. Use these to help your dog make the transition into the group of dogs that is already there: generally, it's best to keep your pet on-lead as you enter the holding pen, then remove it before your dog meets the other dogs already running free.

Never let your dog simply run with the other dogs while you chat on the phone. She needs you to be involved, or she will simply ignore your existence while having a great time with her own species. This can damage all the training you have put in.

Most owners who frequent their local dog park do so regularly, and this means that you will start to recognize familiar faces if you go at the same time each day. This can give your dog a chance to make canine buddies that she feels safe playing and socializing with. However, beware of allowing your dog to become part of a 'gang' that is hostile to other dogs, or allowing her to practise unruly behaviour, which may then become a habit.

Your dog's recall may not be quite as pristine in the dog park as it is at home, and she may not always want to leave the park when you do. Practise getting her to come when called in the park, and then allowing her to run free again. In this way she'll never know when it's really time to go home.

Code of conduct

The following rules are common to most dog parks:
* Owners are legally responsible for their dogs and for any injuries or damage caused by them
* Pick up all dog waste
* Keep your dog on-lead while entering and exiting the dog park and always carry a lead
* Limit three dogs per person in the off-lead area
* Supervise children closely
* No children under eight years of age
* Do not bring food or glass into the off-lead area
* Never leave your dog unattended
* All dogs must be licensed and vaccinated
* No dogs in heat
* Closely supervise intact males
* No puppies under four months of age
* Owners must stop dogs from digging and fill any holes created by their dogs
* Prevent your dog from bullying or fighting other dogs – no exceptions.

solving common
problems

jumping up

Dogs jump up at people for a number of reasons, but even where their intentions are friendly, it can cause havoc on the city streets and devastate your social life. No one likes being jumped on – least of all when wearing their best city suit or dressed up for dinner – but for children and the elderly, jumping up can be a safety risk.

It is important to understand that dogs nearly always jump up in order to be social, so to deal with this in a negative way will undoubtedly impact on their relationships and their views of people.

Sit to greet

If you have a young puppy, prevention is ideal. This simply requires a consistent approach – each and every time your dog greets someone, ask him to sit before being petted. This works wonders because it is physically impossible for your dog to jump and sit at the same time. However, it has the added benefit that you can praise and reward him for doing the right thing, rather than nagging him for 'bad' behaviour.

Make sure that your dog understands the 'Sit' command first (see pages 76–77). Keep some food treats at strategic points where you know that he might be tempted to jump up, and ask him to sit when greeting all members of the family and familiar friends. Be generous with your rewards and praise for sitting – it's difficult for many dogs to resist temptation!

You can also encourage visitors – and even strangers in the city – to help you train your dog. To make this work, you need to employ some human psychology. Keep a toy, such as a hollow chew toy stuffed with food treats, by the front door. Be prepared by putting your dog on a lead if you can predict when someone will arrive. When someone comes to the door ask them if they would help with your dog's training by giving him his special toy. However, tell them that he must sit first in order to get it. Magically, this seems to make even the most harried visitor into an instant dog trainer – they keep hold of the toy until your dog is sitting, whereupon he receives the toy as a reward for good behaviour and not jumping up.

Fetch!

Many gundogs are highly social and love to leap all over people. However, send them to fetch a toy and this miraculously seems to stop them jumping up.

Rehab for jumpers

If you already have a problem with your dog jumping up, then consistency is the key. Most dogs jump up to greet people and to get attention. If this works then they will pursue the habit for ever. Follow the programme below to create zero-tolerance of jumping up, but still enable your dog to enjoy greeting people.

1 If your dog goes to jump up, turn away and fold your arms. Make this an Oscar-winning performance of disgust. It gives a strong, clear signal that he will not get any attention.

2 Don't say anything, look at or talk to the dog until all four feet or his bottom are firmly placed on the floor. You may need to be persistent with this.

3 Praise and pet him only when all his feet are on the floor or when your dog is sitting. You can give a food treat and lots of attention to reward good behaviour.

running off

Dogs love to run – they run because it feels good, want to get away from something or because the motivation to reach something is stronger than staying with you. Unfortunately, running off in the city can be dangerous, and losing your dog is every owner's worst nightmare. If your dog is inclined to wanderlust, prevention is always better than cure.

the sight or sound of the city, keep him on a lead for safety and gradually expose him to events by taking him out little and often, or by seeking help from a professional behaviour specialist.

Running towards

The vast majority of dogs that run away from their owners on walks are actually running *towards* something that they find more fun, interesting or rewarding. This is not necessarily a personal insult – after all, it's hard to compete with the attractions of their own species, or with a highly exciting chase prospect, such as a squirrel. However, the more work you put in to teaching your dog that it is worth coming when you call, the more rewarding his responses will be. If your dog goes selectively deaf in the dog park, or pretends he can't see you when you have the lead in your hand, taking the time to teach a whistle recall might be the answer.

Running away

Just like many other animals, when faced with a threat, a dog's two main coping strategies are flight and fight. Fearful or anxious dogs will nearly always choose flight, and this means that they are particularly vulnerable to running off if they are startled by a sudden loud noise or by a sight with which they are unfamiliar. For this reason alone, it is worth socializing your dog to all the unexpected experiences that the city has to offer while he is still young. If your adult dog is inclined to flee at

Benefits of using a whistle

Teaching your dog to respond to a whistle has several advantages over relying on your voice alone:

* The sound of a whistle carries further than your voice, especially in windy conditions.
* A whistle does not convey emotion, such as frustration, anger or fear.
* A whistle is transferable between handlers, ensuring that the dog returns to whoever is walking him.

Whistle recall

Dogs do not automatically respond to a whistle (even 'silent' ones), but need to be 'tuned in'. For this exercise you will need your dog's food in a bowl, a whistle and your dog, wearing his collar.

1 Get your dog to sit – most dogs sit automatically if you raise the food bowl above their head. Then put a finger in your dog's collar for gentle control.

2 Put the food bowl on the floor, telling your dog to 'Leave'. Get him to wait for a couple of seconds.

3 Now blow the whistle for three short, sharp blasts. Release your dog's collar to let him eat. Practise this at each meal for at least a week to form a strong whistle/food association.

Perfecting the recall

You can then build up to using the whistle to call the dog to you indoors. At mealtimes, get a family member to hold your dog in another room. Use the whistle signal. Your helper should then release the dog, which comes running and gets his dinner. As the dog grasps the idea, ask for a sit on his return and hold his collar before giving him the food, as this ensures he doesn't just return, grab the food and shoot off again. After about two weeks of training, you can build up to practising outside in the dog park or safe city park, with your dog on a long line.

stealing items in the home

Does your dog pick up tissues and then run under the kitchen table with them? Do you see your possessions being purloined and removed to the garden or back yard to be chewed? Does your dog sneak into the kitchen and steal your packed lunch before you leave for work in the city? You are not alone!

Think like your dog

There is one main reason why dogs steal items in the home: because it's fun! If you have this problem with your dog, it is essential that you think about it from his point of view – not from your own.

There your dog is, lying on the floor, chewing a dog toy. He's being good and well behaved, but what happens? Nothing. This behaviour gains little or no response from you. He gets a bit bored, so he gets up, wanders around and discovers the TV remote control. He picks it up. What happens? Suddenly he is engaged in the most exciting chase game in the world!

Clearly, an intelligent dog will soon work out that being well behaved is dull, while stealing something of value results in the doggie equivalent of a lottery win, in terms of fun and attention. Simply by trial and error he will soon discover that the more value an item has to a human, the better the game – hence TV remote controls, reading glasses and wallets are often favourites. However, other items are not immune. If an owner leaps up and down and 'barks' encouragement over the theft of a tea towel, scrap of paper or even a stone in the garden, the pup's response will be pretty much the same. In this way, puppies learn to attract their owner's attention and encourage them to 'play'.

Once this has happened a few times, however, owners can start to become unaccountably aggressive – at least from the pup's perspective. One minute the human is chasing the pup around the house, and the

next they are forcibly removing the item from his mouth, making growling sounds and causing discomfort. Next time, a clever pup will dive under the dining-room table to avoid being caught.

Anti-theft strategies

Overall, the lesson is to ignore or distract your puppy in the early stages of 'stealing games' and to pay him attention when he is chewing the right kinds of objects. Teaching a reliable retrieve (see pages 132–133) can also be a simple way of reducing conflict. A dog that enjoys fetching objects to you for rewards and praise will never need to run off with them in the opposite direction. Try the following strategies.

* Put away items of value. Make sure that your puppy cannot get hold of your most precious things. Puppies especially love socks, pens and shoes.
* If your pup picks up something he should not have, but which you can sacrifice, then do so and ignore it. Tissues, tea towels and twigs can all be ignored. Stand up and walk out of the room to show you really don't care. This can have the most dramatic impact and can prevent a puppy from making the wrong associations between possessing objects and having fun.

Many gundogs need to follow their instincts by fetching an item to you when you come home – make sure toys are available, or it could be your favourite shoes!

* If you cannot walk away, do not chase your puppy for the item, or shout. Call him to you, praise him and give him a titbit in return for the item.
* Work on teaching your dog to fetch items to you. This utilizes his natural instincts.

Feng shui away

If you have been used to living in a clutter-free environment, you may have to alter your perspective when a dog moves in. Dogs need to chew – it helps them to relax and keeps them occupied when you are not there. Providing multitudes of chew toys may make your home resemble a well-stocked nursery school, but it's worth it to keep your home intact.

pulling on the lead

Does your dog pull so hard on the lead that you worry he is going to choke himself? Are you reluctant to take him out for a walk because it's such a struggle to control him in the crowded city streets? Pulling on the lead is a major problem for many owners, but there are many steps you can take to ease the problem.

Train your dog!

The most obvious solution is to train your dog not to pull on-lead. Remember that dogs pull on the lead primarily because we reward them for doing so, simply by going where the dog wants us to – and at his pace.

Follow the training section to get your heelwork practice under way (see pages 84–85). Unfortunately,

pulling on the lead is so rewarding for dogs that it is not something they grow out of. Indeed, the more practice they have at the behaviour, the better they get at it, so start now before your dog has a chance to practise for even one more day.

Bear in mind that some breeds are more prone to pulling than others. Staffordshire Bull Terriers, Bull

Terriers, Boxers and Siberian Huskies are all expert 'steam trains' when it comes to pulling – indeed, their genetic background encouraged this ability and made use of it to pull carts and sleds.

Quick-fix equipment

If your dog is a truly persistent puller, then using a correctly fitted head collar such as a Gentle Leader or a body harness can give your training a better window of opportunity – especially in the city where instant obedience is often required. Consistency is important in this exercise, so this is one way in which you can try to ensure that your dog never gets the chance to pull. These are aids, however, and should always be used in conjunction with training.

Choke and check-chain collars or prong collars are unnecessarily punitive and can cause severe damage to your dog and relationship. Instead, commit time and effort to your gentle on-lead training and you will soon see results.

Wise up

Be honest, and ask yourself just how much time and effort you have put into training your dog not to pull on-lead when you are not actually trying to walk him in the city streets. You wouldn't try to teach your dog a complex new trick amid the hustle and bustle of the city; instead, you would work on it at home in peace and quiet, and only when you had perfected it

there would you practise it in a more distracting environment. The same goes for on-lead training.

* Put in time and practice at home, and in quiet areas of the city, teaching your dog not to pull on-lead. Do not expect this to be an instant cure – most dogs find it rather dull, unless you make it rewarding to walk nicely rather than pull.

* Use sanity-saving equipment that is kind to your dog as well as gentle on your arms. Head collars and some body harnesses for dogs can work well, particularly with big, strong dogs or those with a low centre of gravity, such as Basset Hounds.

* Find a good training class to give you some support and help. Check it out before you attend to make sure the methods used are kind and gentle, and be prepared to do your homework.

You wouldn't walk a horse on a collar and lead, so why a dog? Head collars work like power-steering for dogs and can save your sanity.

barking

Perhaps the number-one complaint about dogs from city dwellers is barking. Of course to our dogs, barking is a natural means of communication, but in high-rise society this will get you blacklisted faster than any other misdemeanour. If you want to keep good neighbourhood relations, check often that your dog is keeping the peace while you're away from home.

Working out the cause

Stopping or preventing a dog from barking can be quite a challenge. It is never as simple as shouting or scolding – both of which must seem just like barking encouragement, from the dog's point of view. Exactly how much your dog barks, the triggers, when, where and why will vary hugely and may, or may not, equate to a problem.

Frustration and boredom

Problem This category covers all those dogs left out in the garden or back yard to 'do their own thing'. It is probably the most preventable, and – from your neighbour's point of view – the most infuriating form of barking problem. Many dogs left outdoors alone will bark in an attempt to call their owners back to them, to gain contact with other dogs or people in the area, or simply just for something to do. The problem is that it becomes self-rewarding and, like other addictive habits, quickly becomes established as a pattern of behaviour.
Solution Give your dog more human company, exercise and mental stimulation (see pages 128–129).

Barking can be an expression of joy, or a demonstration of fear. The dog's body language will give you clues as to how he is feeling.

Territory guarding

Problem Humans are contrary creatures. Most of the time we loathe the sound of barking – especially when it's coming from someone else's dog. However, from time to time we positively applaud it. Most dogs bark at the front door or when a car pulls up outside the house, and this seems to be within most owners' acceptable parameters. However, if your dog continues to bark incessantly once your visitor is in the house, or often barks when there's actually no one there, you need to implement some retraining.

Solution Do not encourage your dog to bark at the door. Instead, give him a treat for running to another room and being quiet.

Attention seeking

Problem Attention seeking has to come high on the list of reasons why many dogs bark. This is hardly surprising – after all, they soon work out that humans find it difficult to ignore barking, particularly if it is aimed directly at them. We reward the behaviour by looking at them, talking to them and touching them.

Solution Ignore the barking and walk out of the room, rather than risk giving your dog unintentional rewards.

Fear

Problem Of course dogs bark as an expression of their emotional state – and no emotional state is as obvious as fear or aggression. Barking may be used as a defence strategy to keep someone or something at bay. It may also be used as a threat to warn another being that further aggression might follow, if the barking goes unheeded. Simply trying to address the barking is like attempting to cure the symptom without considering the disease.

Solution Increase your dog's confidence by rewarding brave behaviour rather than fear. Seek professional help if your dog seems excessively anxious.

Fun

Problem Just like kids, dogs can't be quiet all the time. There are occasions when barking is a sheer expression of joy and excitement. Some breeds like to bark more than others: whether as alarm-givers, prey-finders or cattle-herders, they love the sound of their own voices and gain genuine pleasure from the action of barking. If you own a breed such as a Samoyed, don't be surprised if his main way of communicating involves being loud and repetitive.

Solution Find places – away from the city, if necessary – and times when you can allow your dog to let off steam and bark. At other times, use distractions and teach him calm behaviour.

fear of people

Does your puppy back away from people he doesn't know, stare at them or growl to make them go away? Does your dog hide behind you in the street to keep away from unfamiliar people or to avoid being touched? Fear is a natural instinct, but it is also a classic symptom of under-socialization and can make life miserable for a city dog.

Defence strategy

Sadly, dogs that feel threatened by the unwanted advance of another dog or person may try to hide, run away or bark to make them back away. Of course, this is an incredibly successful strategy, because once the threat retreats, the dog instantly feels better. Indeed, this feeling of relief is one of the most powerful reinforcers, or rewards, that exist and means that the dog will simply repeat the behaviour in any future circumstance where it feels worried.

Unfortunately, even puppies of 12 weeks old can look quite scary when they are barking as a defence strategy, and it takes experience and practice to ignore it. Humans tend to want to look at a puppy that is barking. They may make tiny, subconscious movements away from it or, worse, try to approach, making reassuring noises. All this can exacerbate matters. In the meantime, the poor owner of the barking pup is desperately attempting to calm him down, which only serves to reinforce the behaviour further.

Treatment for fear problems is a highly complex area that needs specialist guidance and support. However, when the dog is still young, there is a huge amount that you can do.

Feel the fear

If you have a puppy that is fearful, the message is simple, although the practice is not. Take your puppy out and about in the city as much as you can. Your dog is in need of *more* exposure to the

big urban world, not less. Set up situations where you meet friends or relatives out and about, or for lunch in your home or theirs. Try to ignore all fearful behaviour completely, and even hand the lead to your friends rather than hold it yourself. Fearful dogs will nearly always try to take comfort and security from their owner, and you must not be part of his successful strategy. Ignore all barking and reward brave behaviour, by marking any confidence with a word such as 'Brave' and giving a treat. Your friends can help by initially ignoring your pup, then by offering delicious treats to reward any brave reaction to them.

Ask relatives and friends to babysit your pup in their own home to build his confidence and spread his loyalties. This can work wonders, because you are not there to inadvertently reward your dog's fear. Most pups quickly realize that good things come from other people, too.

Ignore the fearful behaviour

In circumstances where a puppy is barking at strangers or other dogs in a fearful fashion, it is essential that his strategy fails completely. This means that the other person, or dog, needs to stay still, and the owner needs to pretend that nothing is happening. In other words, all parties ignore the barking completely. This can be difficult to achieve in an urban situation where strangers are in a hurry and may not act exactly as you would ask. For this reason you need to set up situations where people who know and understand how to react can help you. A good dog-training class or behaviour specialist may be the answer here, or ask for assistance from other dog owners.

Most of all, don't sit at home and ignore your puppy's fear problem. It needs to be addressed as soon as possible. It will *not* go away on its own, and may increase to the point where your dog doesn't want to go out in the city.

Taking your puppy out and about to meet the city is an important part of preventing and overcoming anxiety.

fear of loud noises

The city is full of car horns, stereos, police sirens, people talking and shouting, loud crashes and even the occasional sound of fireworks, cars backfiring or thunder. To our dogs, this cacophony must be almost overwhelming. Many dogs experience stress and anxiety when startled by such occurrences and look to us for reassurance and how to behave.

Exposure to city sounds

A fear of loud noises is a natural response for dogs in the wild – it keeps them safe and ready for action if they are suddenly threatened. As a result, our dogs have to learn to overcome this natural reaction and ignore all the weird and wonderful noises the city has to offer. It is essential that this process begins before the dog reaches 12 weeks, or the critical window of opportunity will be closed.

The priority is that your puppy meets the city, and that he is simply exposed hundreds and hundreds of times to the noisy world he is now living in. During these exposures, you should watch his body language closely. Your puppy should appear relaxed and confident. If he reacts to a sound, by cowering, shaking, barking, jumping up or whining, ignore it completely. This is far more difficult than it sounds, because human instinct dictates that we want to reassure our pup, cuddle him and talk to him. Even if you understand the importance of ignoring fearful behaviour, other people may not – so beware of strangers inadvertently undoing all your good work.

Anxiety strategy

Over a period of time, your puppy should be less and less reactive to the sounds the city throws at him. After many hundreds of exposures, your dog should appear confident at all times and, even if suddenly startled by an unexpected noise, should recover quickly and continue as if nothing has happened. Try the following tactics when you start out.

* Watch your pup carefully while you are out and about exposing him to city sounds. If you detect any signs of anxiety – such as his ears going back or his tail going down – stand still.

* Make it clear that you are ignoring him completely all the time he is feeling anxious. Fold your arms and look away from him.

* As soon as your pup recovers and seems confident again, you can continue on your way, still without making a fuss – it's all just part of daily life. Remember: ignore fearful behaviour; reward bravery. It is far more difficult for humans to do this than dogs, but it is essential training for urban living.

It may be natural for your pup to be startled by an unexpected sound, but how you react will determine his long-term response.

Sounds scary

For dogs that really seem to be suffering from being bombarded by the sounds of the city, you can gradually build their confidence through a process known as 'desensitization'. CDs and DVDs are now available containing many different sounds that your dog needs to learn to accept in daily life. These are meant to be played in the background at home, at a level just low enough that your dog doesn't react. As he becomes accustomed to this, you can gradually increase the volume, so that the noise is simply a background to his daily life. Over a period of days and weeks your dog will become so used to the sounds that he is no longer phased by them outdoors.

This method can work well, but do bear in mind that some frightening noises are accompanied by other factors in 'real life' – for example, thunder is often preceded by a change in atmospheric pressure.

mounting other dogs

Without doubt, this is one of the most embarrassing behaviours a dog can perform, especially with a city audience! Dogs mount other dogs – and occasionally cushions, or human legs or arms – for several reasons, not all of them sexual in motivation. Although males are far more likely to engage in this behaviour, females also use it as a dramatic social signal.

Experimental mounting

Puppies of both sexes may engage in mounting behaviour, with both live and inanimate victims. Many owners report that their puppy mounts cushions, favourite soft toys or other items – and while this seems most common in male puppies, which are clearly experiencing an increase in testosterone, it is by no means confined to them.

Puppies also experiment with mounting each other when playing – they will target either end and seem unstrategic about how, and who is the victim. On the whole, this kind of mounting behaviour is just 'testing the water' and disappears as the puppy gets older. However, laughter or attention of any kind can cause it to become a learned behaviour, so it is best to either ignore it, or remove the 'object of desire'.

Mounting as communication

Adult dogs will sometimes mount other dogs, even if they have no true sexual motivation. This is far more likely to be a form of social interaction – where one dog wishes to exert authority over another or has simply become over-excited. On the whole, other dogs do not take kindly to this behaviour and may snap or show aggression to warn the mounting dog off. If your dog persists in this behaviour, neutering can be an option, although this should be discussed with your vet. If he is already neutered, try to identify which dog yours picks on – it may be that he is bullying or disciplining another dog, which may require specialist help to resolve.

Mounting may be embarrassing for owners, but it is a natural part of reproductive and social behaviour for dogs.

home-alone
hound

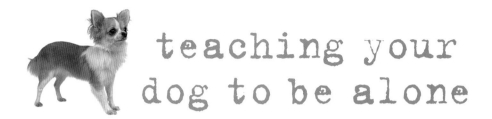

teaching your dog to be alone

Dogs are social animals, and in the wild they would rarely be alone. This means that we have a responsibility for teaching our dogs to be at home alone while we are out in the city. The easiest time to do this, of course, is while your puppy is still young. However, establishing a routine can be useful for older or rehomed dogs, too.

Prevention is better than cure

There is nothing as upsetting as seeing a dog that you love in total distress when you leave her at home alone. Dogs may bark, howl, urinate or defecate in distress or protest. They can also do extensive damage to your home in your absence, chewing or scratching in their efforts to escape or to find some relief. Dogs have been known to break out of cages and jump through windowpanes in order to reach their owners. This kind of suffering is clearly problematic for both your dog and you, but in the city it can also impact on neighbours and may even get you into trouble with your landlord or local authority if your dog is running riot in your neighbourhood.

There are a number of factors to consider when teaching your dog to cope with being alone at home. She needs to be both physically comfortable and emotionally secure. She also needs to know and understand a routine, which she will then simply accept as a part of everyday life. For this reason, it is a good idea to start leaving your puppy for short periods even in the first week that she is with you in her new home. Many owners make the mistake of taking two weeks off work to welcome their new pup, and then spend every waking minute with her for that fortnight. Unfortunately, they have to go back to work and school, and the puppy is suddenly left alone – inconsolable.

Practise leaving your pup

Start by making sure that your puppy is tired. Give her some exercise or a good game, and wait until you see signs that she is becoming sleepy. Place her in the area where she will be sleeping when you leave her – her bed or an indoor crate (see pages 42–43) if you are using one – and calmly and quietly leave her there. A baby gate can be useful to keep her in one room if you are not using a crate. Now you can potter about in the rest of the house or apartment, or you can pop out for just a few minutes. If your puppy whines or cries, do not rush back to her. Instead, wait a while to see if she stops and settles down. This can take 10–15 minutes. Once your pup has settled, leave her there on her own for up to an hour, then return. When you do so, keep your homecoming calm and quiet. Be matter-of-fact about letting her out and taking her out to the toilet straight away.

The main points to watch are:

* Make sure your dog has had exercise and has been to the toilet. She won't be able to settle if she's feeling uncomfortable. Give her a comfy bed or crate to rest in and encourage her to use it at other quiet periods, when you are there with her.
* Give your dog plenty of exciting interactive toys and chews, such as Kongs, Buster™ Cubes and activity balls, and teach her how to play on her own (see pages 128–129). This is essential because even well-balanced dogs get bored and need to chew.

* Leave your dog calmly and return without fuss. She should come to regard you going out as a normal part of her daily routine. Leave her little and often, especially in the first few weeks. This will help to build her confidence that you will always return.
* Never punish or scold your pup on your return – even if she has made a mess or chewed something she shouldn't – it will only make her more anxious next time.

Chewing is an integral part of normal dog behaviour – but what your dog chews is down to you.

establishing a routine

Dogs accept being left by themselves far more readily if they understand there is a routine, which means that their owner will eventually return to them from their ventures into the city. You can help your dog grasp this by giving her ways to predict what is happening and by making her feel secure.

Visual signals

All animals (including humans) use signals in communication. These help us to predict what is happening, and what we should do in response, reducing frustration and stress. Traffic lights are one example of this: we see the green light and know that we can move ahead safely; we see the red and, although we may feel slightly frustrated, we stop – no matter how much of a hurry we are in.

Dogs respond well to visual signals in the environment because they are designed to look for changes that might indicate threat, food or a chance to be social. You will already have noticed that dogs see even tiny changes in us and our behaviour – such as which pair of shoes we are putting on, or whether we are going into the kitchen to make a cup of coffee or to get her a biscuit.

Teaching a traffic-light system

Using a visual signal to tell your dog that you are going out means that she will resign herself to a short period alone without experiencing frustration. Once she learns the signal, it can also be used when you are at home to tell her that you are 'unavailable' and will give her your attention later on.

What gets rewarded will be repeated. Praising your dog for accepting the routine is an important part of training.

Your signal needs to be visually clear, and easy to move. This is because you will put the signal up each time you are preparing to leave the house, and take it down again once you come home. The signal could be a towel, hung over an internal door handle; a large Post-it note stuck to the front of the fridge; or a windchime that you hang up by the front door as you leave.

How to teach your dog the signal

Establishing a clear signal for your dog will reduce her frustration and any potential anxiety about you leaving. It is vital that the whole family is consistent in using the signal, so keep it by the front door or by your keys, so that you are prompted to remember it whenever you leave your home for the city. Dogs that learn clear signals tend to be calmer than those that have mixed signals going on around them. This is true of all your training, not just teaching your dog to be home alone.

Each time you are preparing to leave your pup, put up the signal, with her in sight. It is important that she notices you doing this, but there should be no fuss involved. Take her to her rest area and give her a Kong stuffed with food, or a chew for her to enjoy while you are out. Leave calmly and quietly. As soon as you come home, remove the signal and put it away somewhere the dog cannot see it or hear it.

Watch your dog over a period of days and weeks. As she learns the significance of the signal she will start to make preparations for being left – such as taking herself off to bed, lying down or going and getting a chew and settling down with it. Bear in mind that dogs are intelligent animals. It is not uncommon for a dog to work out that the signal means she will be left alone, only to deliberately remove it if she gets the chance, so keep it well out of reach.

Seek help

Never, ever punish your dog if she has behaved badly while you are out. This will only increase her anxiety and lead to more problems in the long term. Seek help early on if you suspect a problem, and check regularly with your neighbours to make sure your dog is not causing a nuisance to other city dwellers in your absence.

mental stimulation: brain games

Keeping your dog entertained while you are out in the city can present a challenge, especially if she already delights in chewing skirting boards or carpets. Simply hoping that your dog will be content with a squeaky toy for four hours is not enough: dogs first need to learn how to problem-solve and enjoy puzzle toys while you are with them, before they can go it alone.

Problem-solving

In the wild, dogs hunt for food, scavenge for berries and search for water to drink. Their day is filled with activity – and sleep. In our world, most city dogs are effectively unemployed. They are given food to eat from a dish, are taken for a walk when and where we decide, and have water on tap. Clearly, the metropolis also places restraints on our dogs' outlets for natural behaviour, and this means that we need to provide mental stimulation in the form of puzzles and games if they are not to become 'self-employed'.

Teaching your dog to solve puzzles may take a little time and patience, and for this reason it is wise to start the process while you are with her. Of course, once she is 'hooked' you will be able to leave her to occupy herself when you can't be there.

Most dogs just love the challenge of a puzzle – it must be the canine equivalent of sudoku.

Scatter-brain

This puzzle is based on the dog's ability to find food even when it is scattered over a wide area. If you offer a dry food, you can get your dog to search for it both indoors and out. Simply take handfuls of your dog's dry food and toss them so that they scatter over a wide area. Send your dog to find every last bit.

If you feed a wet food (such as tinned food), you clearly cannot throw it around the home. However, you can use it to fill a chew toy, such as a Kong, by squashing it in with a spoon. In that way your dog will have to work at the toy to get the food out.

Under the cup

Ask your dog to sit while you place a dry food treat under an old upturned cup or mug. Tell her to find the treat, then let her work out for herself how to get it.

Dogs have different ways of approaching this dilemma. Some will use their paws to push the cup over, while others will use their nose or teeth to move it. Some genius dogs have even been known to pick up the cup by the handle to get at the food! It's important that you let your dog work out how to solve this puzzle. If she gives up, simply lift the cup a tiny bit so that she can see the treat again, to renew her interest.

Once your dog has got the hang of solving this puzzle, you can make it more difficult by placing the cup on different surfaces, or by using more challenging items to cover the food, such as a cardboard box or an old, heavy bowl. These safer options can then be left for your dog to work on in your absence.

Scatter-feeding is a useful way to encourage your dog to express natural foraging behaviour.

mental stimulation: chew toys

Now that your dog has learned to use her brain, it's time to employ her skills so that she is kept busy while you are out in the city. Dogs that are occupied are more likely to sleep, too, meaning that your neighbours are kept happy. Chew toys are the most practical means of employing your dog's instincts while keeping her content.

Chewing

Chewing objects is a natural stress-reliever for dogs. Adolescent dogs especially need to do this, simply to feel calm and to relieve tension or discomfort in newly erupted teeth. The consequences of failing to provide enough attractive chew toys for your dog can be severe. She may view your furniture, rugs, even walls and skirting boards as giant chew toys – and this will have consequences for your relationship with her quite apart from the cost.

There are many chew toys on the market, and they vary in type, price and effectiveness. Although all dogs are individual in their likes and dislikes, there are certainly some that appeal to dogs more than others. You may need to try several before discovering your dog's favourites.

Kong: king of chew toys

The Kong toy is a joy for city dogs. A hollow rubber pyramid, it bounces off in different directions and enables the dog to play by mouthing, chewing and chasing it. As it is hollow, you can fill it with delicious foods; and as your dog chews on the toy, she is rewarded by small pieces falling out. The toy is made from natural rubber, so it is generally safe even if she chews pieces off, although take care she doesn't swallow any. Monitor your puppy when you first introduce the toy, to ensure it is the right size for her jaw. Kongs come in softer versions for puppies.

Teaching your dog to chew the Kong

There have got to be 101 things a dog can't be doing if she's chewing a Kong: digging through the floor, barking at the neighbour's cat, chewing your new furniture. These toys are marvellous for bored and frustrated dogs, even when you are at home.

Chewing is an essential natural behaviour for dogs of all ages. Provide plenty of chew toys to keep your dog occupied.

When you are loading up the Kong, pick some food your dog really likes. Push this right into the point of the Kong. Cheese (especially individually wrapped slices) is wonderful for this because it moulds to the shape of the Kong. Other suggestions are peanut butter and even Marmite.

Next come the bits that your dog will have to work at to get them out. Ordinary dog biscuits are ideal, because they get crunched up and then fall out of the hole straight into your dog's mouth. Ones that come in different shapes are great because as the dog plays with the Kong, she may suddenly get rewarded by a whole biscuit falling out if she has bounced it along the ground a few times.

Finally, load up a few 'easy pickings' into the top – bits of tasty treat that will fall out as soon as the dog touches the toy with her nose. This gives your dog a chance to realize what rewards are on offer.

Bottle alternative

For a cheap Kong alternative, you can use an empty plastic water bottle (minus the lid). It's important that the plastic is the kind that simply crumples when squashed, rather than splitting, because this could hurt your dog's gums. Pop some pieces of your dog's dry food or a couple of dry dog treats into the bottle, and then let your dog shake it, roll it and even throw it around to get the food out.

Many dogs learn to solve this chew puzzle in the most ingenious ways – throwing it down the stairs is perhaps the most imaginative yet!

physical exercise regimes

One of the most effective ways of preventing, and even treating, separation problems is to make sure your dog has sufficient exercise before you leave her. A short walk round the block may be enough for us before a day in the city, but most dogs need far more in terms of free running, mental stimulation from sniffing and searching, and social interaction to be content.

Retrieving

Giving your dog enough exercise may simply require more time and effort, and this shouldn't be a great sacrifice. After all, the exercise and stress reduction do humans as much good as they do dogs. However, there are some occasions when giving your dog huge amounts of free running may simply not be practical. It may be that your own physical capacity for exercise is limited, or that space in your city is at a premium. In these circumstances, teaching your dog to retrieve can be a simple and practical solution – if she will run after a ball or toy and bring it back to you, the potential for enjoyable, extensive and energetic exercise is limitless.

The thrill of the chase

Don't be tempted to believe that only Retrievers are naturally good at playing fetch games. All breeds can be taught to retrieve, although clearly some will have more enthusiasm than others. Breeds such as Jack Russell Terriers and Cocker Spaniels can be superb retrievers – they love the speed and the thrill of the chase associated with it. It's a great way to encourage more exercise within the constraints of the city.

132

Teaching the retrieve

Some dogs take to retrieving like ducks to water. Others are simply not natural retrievers and take time and patience to learn that it's both enjoyable and rewarding.

Never force an item into your dog's mouth and hope that she will hang on to it. Retrieve training needs to be fun for your dog, or she will do it reluctantly or not at all.

1 Choose an item that you think your dog will like to have in her mouth. Encourage her to show an interest in it by wiggling it and making it appear and disappear, like prey. As soon as your dog takes it into her mouth, say 'Good' and encourage her to come towards you for a treat.

2 Offer the treat so that your dog has to drop the toy in order to eat it. Do *not* snatch the toy, but leave it there until she has finished the treat, then start playing with it again so that your dog wants to hold it once more.

3 Repeat this process until your dog is reliably picking up the toy and coming towards you with it for a treat or a game. Only now can you start to throw it a little distance away, so that she will bring it back to you for a reward.

Perfecting the retrieve

Using two identical toys when teaching a reliable retrieve can also be effective. Once your dog has grasped the essentials of retrieving (see above), throw one toy a short distance, then wait for her to pick it up and bring it back. Throw the other toy immediately. This exercise is great for dogs that are good at retrieving, but are reluctant to drop the toy.

The ideal toy to use for a retrieve game is one that the dog enjoys carrying, but that you can get hold of, too. Balls on ropes are perfect for this, and Kongs on ropes that also float on water are available. Always make sure that balls are hollow and large enough to be safe – your dog could suffocate if she swallows a solid ball that is too small for her.

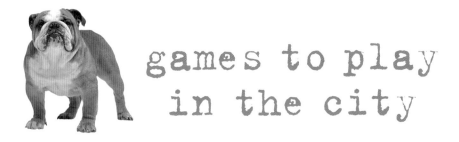

games to play in the city

Although the city may appear to offer few opportunities for exercise, fun or games, this is not necessarily the case. Just as we have to create urban sports and activities for our own enjoyment, so we need to be imaginative when it comes to our dog's need to release pent-up energy. This is an essential prerequisite of leaving your dog home alone when you leave for the city.

Even in highly built-up areas there is often the space for a retrieve game, and this can be made even more exciting by varying the speed and distance of your throws. Some fun gadgets have now been designed to help with this – there are plastic throwing arms that can propel the ball much higher or further than a human hand, and 'catapult' designs that send the ball into the distance.

Frisbee™ fun

If your dog shows proficiency for retrieving, you may consider extending her skills by teaching her to catch a Frisbee™. This is now a big event in many countries, and Frisbee™-catching competitions are common and entrants are judged on the accuracy, distance and style of their abilities. If you wish to play Frisbee with your dog, choose one that has soft edges, to avoid causing

any discomfort to your dog's mouth, and build up her catching skills gradually. Although some dogs become super-athletes in this field and can leap great heights to catch 'trick' throws, it takes time and training to reach this level.

Urban agility

Although it might seem unlikely, your own local environment can provide a playground for your dog. The urban landscape may seem like a concrete jungle to us, but with a little creativity you can teach your dog to see it in a different way. How about mapping out an urban agility course for your city hound?

* **Bollards** A row of bollards or even traffic cones may look like a restriction to us, but can be an opportunity to teach your dog to weave in and out of them consistently: the city equivalent of weaving poles in the agility field.
* **Ramps** Ramps of all kinds can be found in the city – they may be designed for wheelchair access or vehicle use, so watch carefully for any traffic. Once you know that it is safe, use the ramp to teach your dog to walk nicely next to you on-lead, both going up and down. This can be a challenging exercise, but is great practice for those dogs that like to pull on the lead at other times.
* **Revolving doors** These offer the perfect opportunity to teach your dog to stay close at heel. With your dog on-lead, enter the door and let it take you all the way round and out again. Your dog will have to stay close to your heel, due to the restriction of the circular space

* **Narrow pathways** There are plenty of narrow stretches in the city – primarily between the pavement and the road itself. Teaching your dog to walk on the kerb, but never to place a foot on the road, is good practice from a safety point of view and also teaches her balance and agility.
* **Low walls** These make perfect dog walks. Even large dogs can learn to place one paw in front of the other without allowing a foot to come off the wall. This can be great practice for agility training. Use lots of praise and the motivation of a food treat, if you need to.
* **Park bench** This is the most important exercise lesson of all. All dogs should learn that when their owner has had enough, they should lie down quietly and wait while the owner reads the paper or admires the urban view.

Urban agility can be a challenge for your imagination and lots of fun for your dog.

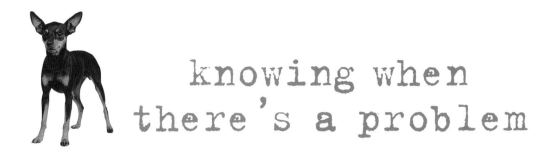

knowing when there's a problem

If your neighbours are starting to complain, or you are coming home to devastation after a hard day in the city, you know that you have a problem with leaving your dog home alone. Although it may appear that your dog is misbehaving just to seek revenge on you for leaving her, nothing could be further from the truth.

Anxiety, fear or fun?

There are many reasons why dogs react badly to being left alone – and although separation anxiety is usually the prime cause, it is by no means the only one. Dogs may experience separation frustration, separation fear, genuine separation distress and even separation fun. Because the problem behaviour is nearly always happening when the dog is on its own, it is risky to guess what the underlying cause is until you have seen the problem actually happening.

For this reason, good early assessment of separation problems is important. You can do this most easily by leaving a camcorder or webcam running on your dog while you are out. This will give you information on your dog's actual behaviour as well as her emotional state. A dog that is having fun while you are out looks very different from one that is miserable. In multiple-dog households, it is not unheard of for one dog to be upset when you leave, while another is fine – so it's important to know which one is actually the culprit and needs your help.

Separation anxiety or mild distress

On the whole, dogs that are showing genuine separation anxiety are over-attached to their owners, sometimes to the point of addiction. Typically, they will want to follow their owner around the house – even into the bathroom – and this is usually focused on one person to whom they are particularly attached.

If you suspect that your dog is unhappy when you leave, or if you recognize that she is a permanent shadow when you are in the house together, then you need to create chances for your dog to practise mini-separations from you when you are actually at home. Put up a baby gate and make it part of your routine that sometimes you are on one side and your dog is on the other. If your dog learns to accept this and begins to relax when you are at home, you will have made inroads into her emotional state when you are out. If your dog cannot cope with this very gentle form of separation, you need to seek specialist advice.

Separation fear

Fear-based problems need to be dealt with sensitively and carefully. Think about how you would treat your dog if she was scared of fireworks. You would ignore her fear, reward brave behaviour and give her a place that was secure and cosy to snuggle in if she felt worried. This approach can work well for fear-based separation problems, too. Try to find out whether there is something in the environment that triggers your dog's fear. It could be noises from the city streets, a neighbour causing disruption or even a fear of thunder or fireworks. For these types of anxieties, professional help is usually required.

Separation fun

Some dogs cause havoc when they are on their own, simply because they can't wait for you to go out to be able to enjoy themselves! Your dog is telling you that she needs more stimulation, exercise and fun in her life. You may find that a visit from a dog walker will help to break up her day, especially if she is being left for prolonged periods. Try to find ways of making sure that your dog is tired when you leave her, and that she has plenty of exciting and novel things to play with. Chews, Kong dispensers, Buster™ Cubes, activity balls and food-scattering games are all made for this type of dog. Go overboard on what you give her to do – otherwise she's got every right to go self-employed while you're out and about in the city.

Most dogs come to terms with being left home alone, but it's important to be realistic – four hours is the maximum for most dogs.

taking action to help

As soon as you are aware that your dog has a separation problem of any kind, it is important that you address it as quickly as possible. If left untreated, separation problems tend to get worse rather than better, and they often lead to suffering for both dog and owner, as well as testing your neighbours' patience.

Consult your vet

The first port of call when you suspect that your dog has a problem should always be your veterinary surgeon. Dogs cannot tell us how they are feeling, and many physical complaints can cause behavioural changes in our pets. Just like us, dogs suffer from stomach ache, muscle pain and possibly even headaches. These physiological problems may make your dog feel irritable, vulnerable or anxious and should not be viewed as bad behaviour, but as issues that need to be treated by your vet.

Talk to your neighbours

Once your vet has given your dog the all-clear from a physical point of view, your next stop should be your neighbours! This is especially the case if you live in an apartment or very close to other people, and is essential if your dog is barking or howling. Such actions cause distress and annoyance to those living nearby, who may not have the same sympathies towards your pet. Simply talking to your neighbours will reassure them that you are aware of the problem and that you are taking action to resolve it. Early communication with those living in the vicinity can prevent conflict and stress later on.

Assess your dog

Your dog's welfare now needs to be addressed. Have a think about the emotional state that may be causing her behaviour.

Separation anxiety or separation fun? An expert opinion is sometimes needed to make an accurate assessment.

Take a look at how your dog behaves when you are at home, as well as how she is when she's on her own. Is she generally confident or does she suffer from other anxieties? Using the guidance given on pages 136–137, you may be able to make some changes that will reassure your pet. However, seeking professional behavioural advice is a highly sensible and successful strategy in cases where your dog's welfare is at stake.

Pets on the couch

Pet-behaviour counsellors and behavioural trainers are usually experienced in dealing with separation disorders. Many work on veterinary referral, because this enables them to act in conjunction with veterinary advice, which may include supportive medication in the worst cases. A pet-behaviour counsellor will nearly always start by assessing your dog through a process of observation, history-taking and background information. Here, evidence from video recordings and testimony from your neighbours can help to build up a comprehensive picture of the problem – and when it occurs. Aspects such as exercise, diet training and medical history will also be taken into consideration.

Once the specialist has assimilated this information, he or she will be able to suggest a behaviour modification programme. Often, this is based on teaching your dog to cope without you by building her confidence and establishing new signals in your routine. There should be no need for punishment or harsh methods with any behavioural programme. Sadly, there is no such thing as a 'quick fix' when it comes to serious behavioural problems. Such programmes often take four to six weeks in the initial stages, but then need to be consolidated over the following weeks and months. Well-devised behavioural programmes are nearly always successful, but they do require time, patience and commitment from the whole family.

The right help

Finding a behavioural specialist who will really be able to address your needs is not dissimilar from finding a human therapist. Make sure that he or she is fully qualified and has had previous experience with similar cases in the past. Recommendation from your veterinary surgeon is by far the best way to seek professional help. Also, have a chat to the behaviour counsellor on the phone before committing to a behavioural assessment. Beware of individuals who claim to be able to 'cure' behavioural problems by punitive methods, or of those who try to persuade you that they should take your dog away for training — your dog's problems need to be addressed in the home.

index

Figures in *italics* indicate captions.

acknowledgements

Executive Editor Trevor Davies
Editor Kerenza Swift
Design Manager Tokiko Morishima
Designer Lisa Tai
Production Controller Carolin Stransky

The publishers would like to thank all the owners and their dogs: Danica and Boo; Katy and Bonnie; Liz and Basil; Rebecca, Ike and Milo; Roz and Amber; Sophie and Dolly; Sue and Millie.

Picture Credits

Commissioned Photography © **Octopus Publishing Group Limited**/Russell Sadur apart from the following:

Alamy Adriano Fagundes 5; Arco Images 63; Gabe Palmer 53; Gari Wyn Williams 4; Guy Moberly 26; ImageState 8; Jonathan Littlejohn 32; Juniors Bildarchiv 33, 102; Paul Mayall 65; Peter Steiner 12; Petra Wegner 37, 66, 115; Juniors Bildarchiv 33, 102; Ilan Rosen 59; tbkmedia.de 61; Isobel flynn 62; Khaled Kassem 68; Key Collection/real.116;
Ardea Jeff Riedel 21; John Daniels 20;
Axiom Jenny Acheson 119;
Corbis Brooke Fasani 29; Dann Tardif 112; Dex Image 108; DLILLC 41; Don Hammond/Design Pics 124; Gabe Palmer 27; Kaufman 94; Lawrence Manning 13; Paul A. Souders 22; Rob Howard 103; Ronnie Sonja Pacho 99;
Getty Bill Deering 117; Dennis Kleiman 71; Greg Elms 11; Lisa M. Robinson 92; Luca Trovato 95; Mark Raycroft 126; Neo Vision 36, 76; Nicki Pardo 139; Noriyuki Yamagashira 17; Rachel Watson 72; Robert Daly 104; Steve Lyne 60; Steven Puetzer 30;
istockphoto Claudio Arnese 24; Peter Mlekuĭ 118;
Masterfile 16; Jerzyworks 138;
Octopus Publishing Group Limited Russell Sadur 49, 52, 54, 58, 67, 96, 121, 130, 136, 137;
Photolibrary 113; Govin-Sorel/Photononstop 87; Heinz Krimmer/voller Ernst 114; HillCreek Pictures 120; Jean Louis Aubert 11; Juniors Bildarchiv 98; Kane Skennar 7, 70; Mirek Weichsel 34; Tamara Lackey 15;
Rex 86;
RSPCA Andrew Forsyth 47, 56; Angela Hampton 88, 122;
Shutterstock Andresr 9, 83, 123; Andrey Nikiforov 35; Carrieann Larmore 144; EML 135; JD 28; Japack Photo Library 39; Jason Osborne 134; Melody Mulligan 35; Michael Zysman 48, 57; Rafael Ramirez Lee 69, 83; luchschen 107; Jacqueline Abromeit 110; Scott T Slattery 125; Tommy Maenhout 132; Vaida 74; Xtuv Photography 93.